BECOMING A

STRATEGIC NETWORKER

The 7 RESULTS Principles
for Building and Leading
a Massive Organization

TONY JEARY
RYAN CHAMBERLIN

Published by Results Faster! and Now You Know Press

Cover design by Thomas Griffin

Interior Design by Adept Content Solutions

ISBN: 978-1-945507-91-5

Printed in the United States of America

Contents

Introduction

You're a leader in the network-marketing industry. You've had some success in building an organization, and yet you're looking to move up—not just to the next level, but all the way to the top. Your goal is to be among the highest income earners in the business. You don't need another "how-to-build-a-network-marketing-business" book. You know the basics; that's how you got to the level you're enjoying now. You're just struggling to find the missing piece of the puzzle that will help you build the massive organization it takes to reach the level you desire. You know you can do it; you just need the right strategy to help you get there. This book is for you.

Literally millions have traveled the network marketing journey to seek financial freedom and their desired lifestyle. As you well know, network marketing is the perfect vehicle and ideal business for anyone who has a dream and is willing to pursue it. Every day, thousands of people wisely choose this opportunity to start their own business, and yet for many something stops them from crossing the finish line to the level of financial freedom that will allow them to live their dreams. Does that sound like your story? On the pathway to success, it takes ambition, passion, determination, and hard work; it also takes the proper strategy and methodologies.

Becoming a Strategic Networker lays out a proven strategy that has helped many people achieve their goals to live the life of their dreams, both personally and professionally. Tony Jeary and Ryan Chamberlin, both considered among the best in their fields, don't purport to have all the answers; however, they have merged their decades of experience, knowledge, and highly successful methodologies and track records to bring you their best practices for getting the results you want. In this book, Ryan and Tony provide a simple, strategic thought process that will transform the way you think, live, and work. It will forever change the way you think about getting results and will increase your effectiveness in all you do.

With two decades of substantial business success and exceptional financial growth under his belt, Ryan Chamberlin has become one of the nation's top network-marketing entrepreneurs. He has trained thousands of leaders in the industry and equipped them with a sustainable system for success, showing them how to leverage their time and maximize their team-building efforts. His systems have helped produce hundreds of millions of dollars in revenue and have resulted in hundreds of people developing six-, multiple six-, and even seven-figure incomes.

Ryan started in the industry in 1993, about a year after his high school graduation, and his early beginnings weren't very impressive. As a matter of fact, he never even bothered to cash his first network marketing check—for $2.01—and it's now hanging in his home office. (He's probably one of the few top earners in the industry who still has their first check, uncashed.) He was with that company for only a few months and never went to any meetings before he dropped out.

In 1995, when he joined his second company at twenty years old, he finally started taking the industry seriously. He often jokes, however, that it took a year to hit the lowest level; he made $47 and was the top earner in his group! That experience, although not profitable, turned out to be a defining moment for him, because that's when he caught the vision for the industry. He started attending weekly events (and some very large events of more than 50,000 people) and absorbing cassette tapes, and he developed an appetite for personal development. That path continued through one other company until 1997, when he and his wife Jenny had their first son. Although at that point he knew it could work, he still couldn't seem to make it work for him; so he decided to quit the network-marketing industry at age twenty-two after three failed attempts.

A few years later, however, while processing mortgage loans, Ryan was re-introduced to network marketing through a friend. This time, at age twenty-five, Ryan decided to give it one more try. With three failures under his belt, Ryan knew what not to do; he just didn't know what to do. For that reason, he focused on making sure he was mentored the right way within his fourth company.

In the beginning he still had a little uncertainty; however, after he had earned his first few checks, his confidence began to build. "I'll never forget when it dawned on me that this was all just a system, and that I could use other people's credibility to fill the gaps that mine didn't have," Ryan said. "I literally saw freedom for my family, which at that time I defined as becoming debt-free and earning $100,000 a year."

Within a few months Ryan was earning several thousand dollars a month. At that point, the company he was with ran a promotion with a large bonus for hitting a certain level. Ryan decided he would do ninety meetings in ninety days. It was his first real ninety-day run, which was another defining moment in his career. The momentum set into motion by that run catapulted his business into over $10,000 a month by the end of the first year. Until then, it had still been a part-time business for him. He went full time, and over the next few years Ryan was able to deposit over a million dollars in commissions—and he was still in his twenties.

That's where the information in this book comes in. Because of his network marketing success, the company he was with began asking Ryan—only twenty-eight years old at the time—to develop systems and trainings for their networkers. For the next seven years, the systems he developed produced hundreds of millions of dollars in volume, earning the Chamberlin family millions of dollars more in commissions. Right in the middle of that time, Ryan met Tony. He and Jenny, at that point, had four boys, whom they homeschooled. They had been stay-at-home parents since they were twenty-six and twenty-five years old and had travelled the world. They had literally enjoyed a large passive income for a decade and weren't looking to disrupt things. They were, however, looking to break through to the next level. Ryan's meeting with Tony turned out to be that breakthrough.

Ryan gives credit to two other experiences early in his career that kick-started his business; a third experience—his coaching relationship with Tony Jeary, The RESULTS Guy™—helped him break through to the next level in the industry.

The first experience happened when he was twenty years old. A friend gave him a box of about fifty motivational cassette tapes from some of the most successful minds of our time, and the principles on those tapes transformed his thinking. The second experience occurred about two years later, when he attended an event at his local church in Belleview, Florida, that featured leadership videos by John Maxwell.

Ryan met Tony while working on a project in Dallas, Texas. He had read Tony's book *Life is a Series of Presentations*, and he made the life-changing decision to hire him as his business coach. One of the first things he shared with Tony was a CD he had produced, entitled "The 7 Laws of the System," which was later developed into Ryan's first book, *Now You Know*. Ryan had been teaching network marketers for years why some succeed and others fail using the same system, and the book is a compilation of those teachings. Tony was so impressed with Ryan's content and speaking abilities that he wrote the foreword to the book. From there, a friendship and business relationship developed that is the stimulus for this book.

Tony Jeary is considered by many Fortune 500 corporate CEOs as a unique business "strategist" and as the *Who's Who* in business consulting and leadership development. Throughout his career he has been honored and blessed to have people seek him out to be their coach—top achievers, such as the president of Walmart, the president of Samsung, the president of Ford, the president of Firestone, the president of TGI Fridays, and even people from the Forbes Richest 400, as well as the Sergeant-at-Arms of the US Senate. Tony also coaches several of the highest leaders within the network-marketing industry, and he noticed many similarities in working with those top leaders and top Fortune 500 leaders. He has also coached on the corporate side of network marketing.

Tony's providential entrance into the network-marketing world came in 1995, when Dexter Yeager invited him to speak to a group of tens of thousands of Amway network marketers. Dr. Robert Rohm, Tony's long-term friend with whom he had co-authored the book *Presenting with Style*, endorsed Tony and recommended him to Dexter and other top field leaders. That was the beginning of an auspicious long-term relationship with many top leaders in the industry. Since then, Tony has worked with corporate leaders and top earners in about fifty of the seventy-five leading network-marketing organizations today.

Working with high-level people with a distinct profile year after year, like Tony has done for decades, has enabled him to pick up distinctions that have a proven track record in bringing about maximum results.

Ryan recognized that Tony had discovered these key elements to success, and that he was inputting life-changing methodologies into leading CEOs and network-marketing leaders around the world that were producing proven results. Ryan's coaching relationships with his network-marketing mentors, and now Tony, inspired him to write a novel called *The Mentor,* which addresses twenty-eight issues every networker must conquer before achieving sustainable success.

About the same time, Tony and his team developed a methodology and shared it with the world in his best-selling book *Strategic Acceleration*, which teaches how to get accelerated results through a formula: Clarity, Focus, and Execution. Ryan read Tony's new book and was motivated by its concepts; so he developed his own strategic blueprint for success and called it *The Rich You Formula*, based upon four elements—a dream, a strategy, actions, and results. Then he co-authored with the late Gary Smalley a book with the same name, which explores those four elements as they relate to obtaining a "rich life" in all areas.

As Ryan's business began to flourish, he realized that his acceleration was primarily a result of the application of principles he had gleaned from Tony. Since not everyone is afforded the opportunity to have The RESULTS Guy™ as their mentor and coach, Ryan asked Tony to team up with him to write a book that combines Tony's success principles with Ryan's networking skills. The result is *Becoming a Strategic Networker,* which combines concepts from Ryan's books, *Now You Know* and *The Rich You Formula,* and two of the most success-generating of Tony's more than forty-five books—*Strategic Acceleration* and *RESULTS Faster!*

RESULTS Faster! is Tony's foundational book and is a compilation of his life's work, laid out in seven core principles that each contain three powerful lessons to help the reader realize maximum results, both personally and professionally. As Ryan was reading the book, he realized that *Becoming a Strategic Networker* could be framed by applying network marketing distinctions to the same seven core principles.

You can see the layout of the book in the strategy graphic on the next page. (Note the inverted pyramid in the back that basically shows the higher you go on the strategy pyramid, the bigger the organization you'll have on the back end.) Each chapter highlights three very important lessons, or what we call strategies, that will lead you to the level of success you desire in each area. You'll end up with twenty-one of what we believe are the most valuable and prolific strategies you can find for building your network-marketing business to the very top level.

Chapter one starts with laying the foundation for a successful network-marketing business by having a *Strategic Mindset* that includes the strategies of beliefs, skills, and results. Then chapters two through four go into the application of Tony's *Strategic Acceleration* Formula—Clarity, Focus, and Execution—in the context of network marketing. By the time you finish this section, you will be able to achieve a higher level of clarity about what you really want by applying the strategies of values, dreams, and goals. With the application of the strategies of MOLO, *High Leverage Activities* (HLAs), and inner circles, you will understand how to *focus* on HLAs that accelerate the results you seek. Finally, you will be more prepared to confidently *execute* your dreams or vision with the network-marketing strategies of posture, action, and momentum.

In chapter five, Force Multipliers, we'll talk about the proliferating effects of these three strategies: tools, events, and recognition. Then in chapter six, we'll discuss the leadership strategies of accountability, communication, and trust. And in the final chapter, Mastery, we'll talk about the strategies of mentorship, your brand, and acquiring the right habits in order to achieve the proven outcomes you desire.

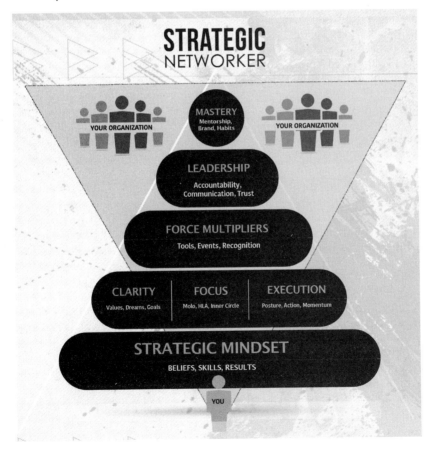

What Ryan and Tony have learned through the years is that most people can become successful high achievers when they get their *why* and *how* questions answered. The *Strategic Networker* mindset will consistently produce results and bring clarity concerning your vision, and then focus becomes a possibility. When you are focused, the capability to execute is realized, and results are the decisive product of a well-executed vision. Great execution flows from great design, and great design is deployed through strategic communication. You will have all of those things by the time you finish reading this book, so let's get started.

## Chapter One

Strategic Mindset: How You Think Determines the Size of Your Results

N etwork marketing is an emotional business. The emotions arise from the most interesting and yet unpredictable source you can imagine, a source that can cause many of your plans to go up in smoke: people. People make our industry unpredictable. Yet, despite the unpredictability, there is a way to navigate to the top of your business. There is a way to create *freedom* in our industry, even though people and their reactions are many times out of your control. There is a strategy!

If your goal is to achieve personal and financial freedom in your network-marketing business, we'll give you the secret right up front: The very best top achievers, those who have extraordinary results in their life, are *Intentionally Strategic* in everything they do, beginning with their *thinking*—which minimizes the unpredictable aspect of their business and gives them more control. In this book, we're going to show you how to do that; that's why we named the book *Becoming a Strategic Networker*. Everything in the book was intentionally and strategically thought out to help you make that giant leap forward and reach the top.

This book was designed upon a set of principles that have not only proven themselves worthy to Fortune 500 CEOs, but have also generated millions of dollars of net revenue for new and seasoned network marketers. You could say this book is really being written to help network marketers learn how *not* to be traditional network marketers—how to think and act differently than a traditional network-marketing book might teach, how to position yourself as the CEO of your own business, and how to recognize a predictable pattern of success in an unpredictable environment.

> **Intentionally Strategic:** The very best top achievers, those who have extraordinary results in their life, are *Intentionally Strategic* in everything they do.

In reality, this book is written for those who have already built a business and want to take it to the next level. And it was written this way so you could not only identify patterns of thinking about each topic from a perspective of success, but also see how the information should be replicated within an organization.

So, as you can see, this is not a how-to-build-a-network-marketing business book. Your company may already have a proven system. This book will tell you how to build a *massive network-marketing business* through *principle-based strategies that work every time.*

Note: As you go through the chapter (and, in fact, through the book), there may be things that you have already learned and put into practice as a leader in the industry. If that's the case, let it serve as a reminder to drive home that particular issue with your organization. You will all be the winners if you do. We encourage you, though, to keep your eyes open for things you read that will seize your attention and give you an "ah-ha" moment that will be a game-changer for you.

Strategic Mindset

When I (Ryan) first launched my network-marketing business, I employed very little strategic thinking. I remember saying to my upline, "Tell me what I have to do, and I'll do it." I was serious, and for the most part it was a simple follow-directions-and-go-to-work mentality that helped me begin my journey. After my team began to grow, however, I quickly realized that without an understanding of a few simple strategies, I was destined to build and keep rebuilding my organization. It wasn't until I lost a few large teams of business and saw my income fluctuate dramatically that I began to ask the tough questions. One such question came after a very sharp top leader who was leaving my organization said to me, "Ryan, you're a great leader, but you're not listening to me. I've been trying to tell you for months now why I'm leaving, and you simply haven't been listening." *What was I not listening to?* It was at that point in my career that I began to listen differently than I had before when leaders were struggling in my business. It wasn't so much what they said but why they were saying it that I was after. And the answers to many of these issues rested mostly in how my leaders thought about the twenty-one strategies outlined in this book.

Tony and I call this having a *Strategic Mindset*, and we believe 100 percent that it will determine the size of the results you're looking for. After all, when I looked around in my early days in the business, I really didn't see too many people who had built their business to last for the long haul of five, ten, or even twenty years or more. How were some people making it big and others not, when they all appeared to be following the same rules? Now, after building teams for over twenty years, and earning a sustainable multiple six- to seven-figure income for most of those years (since I was twenty-six years old), I have identified the *Strategic Mindset* thinking patterns. And much of this identification has come from working with my friend Tony Jeary, a coach to the world's top CEO's.

Since the mind is the engine of action, you ultimately become and do what you think. If the results you're getting in your network-marketing business are less than you want or expect, you need to develop a new way of thinking about what it takes to reach the level of success you desire. To get better results, you have to have better execution, and better execution comes from knowing the right actions to take. And the best way to know what actions to take is to have the right mindset—a *Strategic Mindset*.

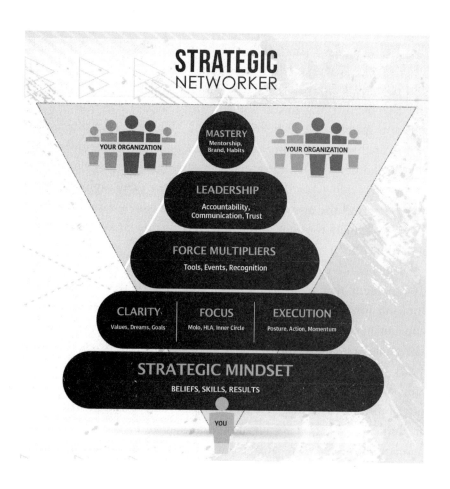

That's why *Strategic Mindset* is at the bottom of our model. Notice that there are two triangles (okay, pyramids, for you network marketers), and that the principle triangle starts with *Strategic Mindset* as the foundation, while the inverted triangle starts with just you.

As you develop strategically through the principles, the primary triangle gets more streamlined and ends with a sharp point at

> **Thinking:** Almost every challenge you and your team will have is a mindset challenge.

mastery. Along the way, and as the principles are developed and embraced, it allows for an organization to naturally grow (inverted triangle) to the point of mastery—without you, despite you, and yet strategically because of you. This book takes you through seven levels of strategy that end in mastery.

As you're striving for mastery in your network-marketing business, you're often faced with challenges that keep you from breaking through that ceiling that's been limiting your progress. We believe that almost every challenge you and your team will have is a mindset challenge. So what do you do when you don't get the results you want, or when you don't get the results you want fast enough? *You make some changes in your thinking!* And we're talking specifically here about the *intentional thinking* it takes to solve problems—to look at all the pieces and make strategic decisions. That means you have to let go of old thought patterns and be open to new ways of thinking to ultimately have a *Strategic Mindset*.

Since how you think affects what you can or can't accomplish, we're going to share with you four kinds of intentional thinking you need to adopt to have a *Strategic Mindset*. These thinking patterns are most common with seven-figure earners in network marketing, so it's good to go ahead and adopt them now.

Strategic Mindset Thinking Patterns of a Strategic Network Marketer

1. No-excuses thinking. You're not after excuses; you're after results.

2. Solution-oriented thinking. Ask "How do I conquer this and go all the way to the top?" instead of saying, "Here's why I can't."

3. Long-term thinking. Look beyond the immediate future, and continually think about what you want to accomplish in this business five, ten, or twenty years from now.

4. Visual thinking. Visualize your success and your team's success.

Of course, there are two kinds of thinking that intentional thinkers must avoid at all costs:

1. Negative thinking. Negative thoughts clutter our minds and derail the intentional thinking process.

2. Over-thinking. This leads to procrastination and low productivity.

So in essence, developing a *Strategic Mindset* can be simple, and yet it can be hard at the same time. It's really about getting intentional and adopting the right understanding of three strategies for your business that you will never stop thinking about, discussing, and communicating to your team. They are: beliefs, skills, and results.

Now let's talk about how your beliefs affect your *Strategic Mindset*. Since having the right beliefs actually provides the foundation for an accurate mindset concerning skills and results, you'll find that the entire chapter has an underlying theme of beliefs.

Strategic Networker Strategy No. 1

Beliefs

Strategy No. 1 VIP: Your belief system ultimately determines the size of your income, the size of your team, and the impact you will have on others.

Whether we realize it or not, we all conduct our lives and make decisions based upon our beliefs. What you believe will determine who you are and how far you will go in life.

Your *Belief Window* Is How You See and Think about the World

One of the most powerful and impactful models that I (Tony) taught Ryan and that we now both teach is called the *Belief Window*. We all have principles and truisms on our *Belief Window* that filter how we see the world, which have primarily been instilled during our upbringing by our family, friends, teachers, religion, and environment. As we go through life, those influences and our experiences, as well as the information we get from the vast media sources around us, keep refining those principles and truisms. All of us are doing life right now the very best we can based on the principles in our *Belief Window*.

Blind Spots

It's important to know our core beliefs, and it's even more important to understand that we can choose new beliefs that will help us be more successful. Sometimes we have some things on our *Belief Window* called *Blind Spots*—those things we can't see about

ourselves and our surroundings—that cause a negative impact on our life and business. Whether our *Blind Spots* are inaccurate principles, missed distinctions, or overlooked perspectives, they hinder our results.

We often illustrate this principle using a picture of a Fed Ex truck. If you're like most people, you've likely never noticed the hidden serving spoon and arrow in the Fed Ex logo, even though you've seen it many times over the years. That's a *Blind Spot* that many people have.

How about the hidden message in the Baskin Robbins logo? The ice cream shop is best known for its thirty-one flavors, so

the BR in the logo actually incorporates the number 31, conveying the message that their customers can enjoy a different flavor every day of the month. Was that a *Blind Spot* for you, as well?

And here's something we all deal with daily: How about the *Blind Spot* in your car? You know, that spot your side mirror doesn't show when a smart little car comes up beside you and passes by your rear bumper and your passenger-side door—the spot you can't see even if you turn your head? Just because you can't see the car, it doesn't mean it's not there. You quickly become aware of that *Blind Spot,* though, when you hear the horn honk as you try to switch lanes.

These examples help prove that we often don't see things that have been right in front of us for a long time. Our experience tells us that if there's an area in your life or your network-marketing business where you're not

> **"" Blind Spots:** Learn to identify *Blind Spots* and correct beliefs that can hold you and your team back from reaching your potential. **""**

getting the results you want, it's very likely you have a *Blind Spot* that's getting in your way. Here are four *Blind Spots* that can hold you and your team back from reaching your potential:

Blind Spots That Stop Growth

1. If you find yourself dealing with the same leadership problems over and over, you may have a *Blind Spot*. For example, early in my career I thought I needed to do everything

for the new distributors who joined my team—all the meetings, calls, etc. I really thought that doing all the work was leadership. That was a *Blind Spot* that was costing me millions. Real leaders equip, empower, and encourage their team members to do the work. They first show them how to do it, then they do it with them, and then they let them do it on their own. Leaders look for opportunities to praise and recognize any positive results their team members achieve in order to encourage more. Your leadership is not measured by what happens when you are present as much as what happens when you're not.

2.   If you're experiencing stress about something out of your control, there's probably a belief getting in your way. Look to see what the belief is. You may have a *Blind Spot*. This often shows itself when someone you view as an asset decides to leave the company you're with and go to another. That happened to me a few times early in my career, and I found myself stressing over it as if I could do something about it. I was literally losing sleep over it, thinking my business was over and not realizing that most of my team was actually still intact. When that kind of thing happens, look at the bottom line—it's *their* decision. It probably didn't happen overnight, and the best thing you can do for your team is to wish those who are leaving the best and move on. If you react and try to get them to change their

> " **Real Leaders:** Real leaders equip, empower, and encourage their team members to do the work. They first show them how to do it, then they do it with them, and then they let them do it on their own. "

decision, more often than not you'll burn a lot of energy and they'll ultimately go anyway. You certainly need to evaluate any mistakes you may have made and vow to improve; then you need to quickly get back to working with those who are ready to accomplish their goals and dreams.

3. If you've sponsored twenty people and still have not created any duplication, you may have a *Blind Spot.*

4. If your income is going down and yet your work load is going up, you may have a *Blind Spot.*

When these things happen, it's important to seek advice. Ask someone you trust to help you figure out your *Blind Spots. Unless we uncover our Blind Spots, there is virtually zero chance that we will adjust our beliefs, and an even lower chance that we will be able to help the members of our team adjust theirs.*

I (Ryan) have had several belief breakthroughs throughout my network-marketing career. At twenty-five years old, I had many *Blind Spots* in my life that were causing me to produce mediocre results. I had never really made money in the network-marketing industry, even though I had sponsored a few people into several different companies. It took me a year to get to the lowest level in the first company I sponsored people into. I got my income up to $47 a month, and I was the top earner in my group—go figure! So how does someone who can hardly sponsor anyone go on to become the top earner in their company? I changed my *Strategic Mindset*, identified my *Blind Spots*, and predominately transformed my belief system.

When I first met Tony Jeary around 2007, I quickly assessed that this coach was different. He not only mentored people on the power of beliefs—he lived it. And even though by that point in my career I had made millions of dollars with one company, I needed some belief breakthroughs (removal of *Blind Spots*) to go to the next level. Tony's influence on my belief system had a huge impact on me—so much so, in fact, that I realized that belief had to be the central component of my third book, titled *The Rich You Formula.*

All four steps of the formula (dream, strategy, actions, and results) are continuously dependent and co–dependent upon a proper belief system. That's why it's so important that we ensure our beliefs are true and accurate and that we root out our *Blind Spots.*

Take the time to write out here the *top five areas* of your business that frustrate you the most. Then, after conversations with your upline and/or mentor, write down two or three *Blind Spots* you've uncovered about how you *think* about these issues. Once you do this, you'll likely be less frustrated with these issues, because you will have uncovered your *Blind Spots* and be focused on your next level breakthrough.

1. _____
2. _____
3. _____
4. _____
5. _____

Blind Spots

1. _____
2. _____
3. _____

Understanding the Belief System of a Massive Organization

Your belief system is really the heart of your network-marketing business. When you understand this, and most don't, you become very strategic and very intentional. Most leaders in network-marketing think their job is to focus on getting more performance out of their teams; their *real job*, however, is to help develop and grow the *belief system* of their team. In fact, what you are really building is a team of believers!

Along with this understanding, there must be certain beliefs that are firmly established in your mind before you can build a massive organization. In all my years of reading and studying about network marketing beliefs, I have never found them simplified better than in the book *The DNA of Business for Network Marketing,* by Eric Golden. Although there are many beliefs we can discuss about this industry, I would like to highlight five (of the eight mentioned in Eric's book) that encompass the majority of the belief issues of an organization, and that you will need to create an entire culture around to support your team. I call them the *Big Five.*

Ultimately, many of the *Blind Spots* you will uncover for yourself and your team will come from the following areas:

The Big Five

1. A belief in the industry

2. A belief in your company

3. A belief in your products

4. A belief in the opportunity this industry provides for you personally and for others

5. A belief in yourself [1]

---

1   Eric Golden, *The DNA of Network Marketing* (Belleview, Now Your Know Press, 2013).

The Industry

The fact is, you must have an unshakeable belief in the industry if you're ever going to build a big business. As you know, our industry is not always held in the most positive light by the masses, because they don't understand it. In fact, the viability of our industry is a huge *Blind Spot* for many people. They don't understand that this is a credible industry and can actually be a better way of doing business than the traditional business model. So when someone joins your organization, their belief in the industry may not be strong enough for them to communicate the true merits of the industry to other people, because they're constantly asking themselves, *Is this going to hurt my credibility?* or *Does it really work?* We've seen some really sharp people with a lot of influence join our industry and then freeze. They can't perform, because they have so many questions about the industry. Until that belief is settled, or until that person has a big enough reason to not care what others think and just go out and make it happen, they're probably not going to perform.

Fortunately, there's a movement in public opinion that's turning our industry into more of a real profession. People are beginning to see that, other than real estate, there's no other independent-contractor industry where individuals can make the kind of money we make—with very little risk in the cost of doing business—and certainly none that can provide the freedom, the flexibility, the time, and the leverage that network marketing delivers. And yet many people still allow the low-cost entry point to illegitimize the fact that this could be a multi-million-dollar opportunity, because it goes against the ingrained social view that a college degree is the only pathway to success.

The person who comes in with the right belief in our industry will see it as if they were actually starting a Fortune 500 business. So many people come into the industry thinking, *I'm going to make a massive profit my first month, and if I don't I'll just shut the doors.* Because of all the rags-to-riches stories this industry has produced, many have developed a lottery mentality (*Blind Spot*) and think if it doesn't happen fast, it isn't worth it. And yet they wouldn't expect those kind of results if they were starting a traditional business. Until they change their thinking and adopt a *Strategic Mindset* that leads them to the right attitude and actions, they're not going to achieve their goals.

The Company

The next belief that must be rock solid is your belief in your company. I have been known to say, "If you have to question anything, you have to question everything." In the world of the *Strategic Networker*, if there is a lack of trust in the ownership or a lack of belief in the product, in customer service, or in the compensation plan, there will not be integrity in the referral. Simply put, a person of integrity cannot refer something they do not believe in. Sure, there are short-term money games out there, and yet this book is not written with those in mind. This book is for the business owner who wants an income-producing asset for generations, not months. Another way to think about this is to consider the values of your company's ownership. Are you in alignment with their values? No company is perfect; however, you need to know whether the owners are committed to always making the company better for the distributors and customers. Do the owners themselves believe in the products? In reality, belief in your company and its values is a game changer. Either you have it or you don't. If your company violates any or all of the four things I just mentioned (trustworthy ownership, believable products, great customer service, or a dependable compensation plan), our advice is to consider finding a new home. If your company scores an A+ in these areas, then the rest of this book will help you develop mastery and reach the top level of your company.

Important note: Many times when someone is not doing the right activity in their business and their personal business is not performing, they tend to blame it on one of the four things above. Thinking you will find the perfect company is a *Blind Spot,* and it is a loser mindset rather than a *Strategic Mindset.* This person will generally not succeed in any company. Be honest with yourself when evaluating your belief in the company you're with.

The Products

Your product belief can come in many ways. Usually, the most powerful is through personal experience. Everyone should be able to highlight a specific personal benefit that one or more of the products you represent currently has for you. Something special happens when a true believer shares their personal experience with someone else. In addition, you can strengthen your belief from the testimonials of others who have used the products. And as you help more and more people, your belief will continue to rise. However, all of this is contingent on your having products that are of high quality and not just something for sale. When a product creates real value for its customers, you have something special. This is one way to differentiate between the short-term-opportunity companies and the ones with real potential.

The Opportunity

Have you attached a strong belief to what's in it for you? One of the most important elements of a successful network marketer is their belief that the right payoff is down the road. Often, people get in for short-term gain, and yet it's ultimately their belief in the long term that keeps them in. As we go through the goals section of this book, it will be important for you to develop the belief that the trade-off for building your network-marketing business is that you can have more of what you want in life.

Everyone has a financial number that can enhance all other areas of their life when their network-marketing business is producing it regularly. What's your number? Is it $1000, $5000, $10,000 or $50,000 per month? Interestingly, coming up with your number isn't really about the money—it's about the lifestyle and freedom. Those who chase the money without purpose never seem to be happy, and those who build for lifestyle seem to be far more rewarded once they arrive. Realize that your strategy, however, is to help people connect "what's in it for them" to the building method of their business; otherwise, they certainly won't keep performing, because it's a business built on inconvenience. It's inconvenient to go out and do meetings; it's disruptive to their family life. So in most cases, unless they have a strong belief that the opportunity provided by this industry will ultimately create freedom for them on the other side within the next year or two, and that they're with a company they can believe in that's aligned with their value system, their performance will decrease and eventually stop altogether.

Belief in Yourself

If you have an unshakeable belief in the industry, the company, your products, and the opportunity, and yet you have no belief in yourself, how far do you think you'll go? You'll make a half-hearted effort, at best, which will get you nowhere. If you're not getting the results you expect—in this business or in any aspect of your life—the common denominator just might be you! You may have habits (like procrastination) based on your lack of belief in yourself, that are sabotaging your efforts. Or you may feel that disappointing results are your destiny; and if that's your belief, they *will* be! As Henry Ford once wisely said, "If you think you can do a thing or think you can't do a thing, you're right"—more evidence that if you want to change your results, you must change your thinking! You're the only one who can do something about it. You must believe in yourself and your ability to make things happen. When you do, you'll find that you'll start to take action, and action is the only thing that brings results. With strategic action, you develop competency. And no matter what business you are in, when you invest in and develop competency you will yield a greater level of belief in yourself and your commitments.

As a leader, you must be constantly building belief in your team in all these areas. When they get all of these beliefs in place—belief in the industry, in the opportunity, in your company, in the product, and in themselves—they'll likely perform at a much higher level, and your organization will see massive growth.

How to Build a Belief-Building Culture

If the right beliefs are at the base of a solid organization, then the next question is, "How can the top leaders in the industry create a belief-building culture that leads to a long-term business?"

They generally get good at two very important things:

1. Eliminating the noise

2. Building a circle of trust

The one thing that constantly challenges and undermines belief more than anything else is noise. Who you listen to matters! With social media, everyone's an expert, and they're all trying to tell you what to do and how to do it. When leaders claim to know what they're doing, they just become one voice among many. You can't listen to ten different people and follow ten different strategies. If you listen to all of them, it will only create confusion, and confusion creates stagnation. Worse, you may go down the wrong path; and in our industry, the wrong path could cost you a couple of years. As a leader in this industry, you must create an environment that teaches very specific things; otherwise, your team will get distracted to the point that they won't perform.

Building a Circle of Trust

So how do you determine who the people are who actually know what they're doing? Who are you going to allow to speak into your life? I (Ryan) have decided that when it comes to many business and life strategies, Tony Jeary is one of the main people I'm going to listen to, because I know how well the things he says have been vetted. I know his track record. If someone says something that contradicts what Tony would say or presents a different strategy, I'm not going to wonder whether Tony's right; I'm going to assume right out of the gate that the other person is wrong, and I'm not going to put a lot of weight to what

> " **Noise:** The one thing that constantly challenges and undermines belief more than anything else is noise. Who you listen to matters! "

they said. I have also decided that my pastor, Jason Varnum, is the person I will seek life and spiritual advice from, and that I will only listen to those in the network-marketing world who have built big, sustainable businesses in harmony with my value system. It's not that I don't hear other things said, or that I don't occasionally get a great idea from someone outside of my sphere; I do, and yet to allow everyone to speak into my life would be chaotic, and therefore unproductive.

So you have to decide—*who is it in your network-marketing business that you're really going to listen to?* Who is it that has what you want and operates with the right belief system that will help you get the results you want? That decision will have a huge impact on your beliefs and your results.

List the three people you have direct connections with whom you will allow to speak into your life within network marketing:

1. _____

2. _____

3. _____

Next, list three non-direct people (example: Tony Jeary, Ryan Chamberlin, your pastor, etc.) whom you will plug into and allow to influence you on a regular basis in life and spiritual direction:

1. _____

2. _____

3. _____

Then once you make these decisions, you have to make another: How much distraction are you going to allow into your life? What you read, watch, and listen to, as well as the people you spend time with, will either push you closer to your goals or push you farther away. They will either fortify your beliefs or cast doubt on them. You become who you run with and what you feed into your mind. Make sure you don't have a *Blind Spot* here. Keep your eyes wide open. And another word of caution: Manipulation of information within our industry is common, and if you're not careful it will destroy your belief in your leadership and in your team. So your job from this point on is to block out the rest of the noise so you can focus.

Raising Team Belief for Momentum

In the last part of this section we want to discuss how top leaders raise the belief within their organizations.

Now remember, how we think *(Strategic Mindset)* about growing the belief of our team will determine our results. So to help you with your effectiveness, I want to share with you four foundational rules for building the belief and the organization we all want. As you're building belief within your team, always remember these rules. In fact, I hope they are constantly swirling around in your head, as they are in mine.

Rule No. 1: You can't make people believe anything—you can only inspire them to want to believe.

So many people are trying to get their teams to believe differently through their words and not their actions. That is not strategic. In reality, it's your words and your actions that matter.

Rule No. 2: Sometimes you have to accept people for where they are and move on.

The sooner you can learn to categorize people's level of belief, the better. Generally speaking, when you sponsor someone, you will quickly be able to assess whether or not they believe in the industry, the company, the products, the opportunity, and themselves, and whether or not they are open to grow. Many people aren't; and if they're not, you shouldn't spend much one-on-one time with them. Instead, drive depth and move on. Realize that unless you want to build your business slowly, every person you spend time with matters. People who have financial breakthroughs in our industry usually uncover the *Blind Spot* that they're spending their time with the wrong people.

Rule No. 3: Never lower your beliefs to accommodate your team.

That is a mistake often made by up-and-coming leaders. They lower their beliefs to accommodate the "lower believer" in a quest to be more relatable and liked. Your team should be influenced to think and believe at a higher level, because one of the attractive forces of a leader is their vision (belief) and how they communicate it. Instead, grow your belief even higher and get better at communicating it.

Rule No. 4: You only need a few.

Understand that you only need a few *big believers* in your team to grow an army of excited people. Don't settle for lower belief, since it dictates the size of your organization.

Once we have these foundational rules as part of our own *Strategic Mindset*, then it's time to raise belief in our team.

How do we do this? Through a system. Those who understand this excel; those who don't usually flounder. Most think of systems as relating only to the sponsoring part of their business, which is definitely a *Blind Spot*. The system we're talking about is a huge part of every aspect of the network-marketing business—sponsoring, growing, and sustaining an organization—and is comprised of business and personal development taught through audios, books, and events. Let's face it, when we can get our team to develop an appetite for growth, they will want to absorb the right information—constantly. They will not resist events, since their belief system tells them they will grow by attending each one; and through growth, they will attract more and more of the right team to help them reach their goals. Between events, they will *want* to absorb the right information, and the right information is material—promoted by people they know, like, and trust—that feeds the proper belief systems. They will understand that the events these people promote are the ultimate re-enforcements of those beliefs. Therefore, it becomes your primary strategy to support and promote such a system in a way that encourages everyone to participate so they can develop a *Strategic Mindset* like yours.

Skills

Strategy No. 2 VIP: Strategic Network Marketers understand that their business is skill-driven; everything you need to be a top leader can be learned.

Our beliefs about the skills needed to succeed in network marketing often become a lid that limits the size our organization can grow to. I (Ryan) have seen incomes get to $20,000 a year and stop, and I've seen incomes get to $100,000 a year and never break past, because this mindset becomes limited. The confusion usually begins with a misunderstanding. I like to illustrate these incorrect beliefs (or *Blind Spots*) common to this industry with teachings that I call "Versus," and I'll start with one that applies to a *Blind Spot* about skills.

Skills versus Personality

Many people think this industry is personality driven, and that only those with an outgoing personality can succeed. Certainly some personalities are more charismatic than others, and yet you will find that some of the quietest people are the largest income earners. A more correct assessment would be that *all* personality types have reached the highest levels of achievement. The point is this: As long as you and your team believe it's personality driven, you will each think that your personality is lacking and will use your flaws as an excuse to hold back. The truth is, this business is skill driven; *everything* you need to be a top leader can be learned.

And if it can be learned, then you can learn it. It therefore becomes a decision, based on whether you *desire* to get out of your comfort zone to improve.

> **Skills versus Personality:** The network-marketing business is skill driven; *everything* you need to be a top leader can be learned.

It really is a matter of stepping out of your comfort zone and identifying the skill sets you need to work on or develop. The good news is that you really only need to develop a *Strategic Mindset* around a few skills.

We've listed below the seven skills that most people are taught when they're learning how to build their business. We actually agree with this list; however, we believe that what is missing is a *Strategic Mindset* about each of them.

Seven Network-Marketing Skills Required to Build a Business

1. Build a list

2. Set appointments

3. Give a presentation

4. Share your product information

5. Follow up

6. Launch new members

7. Duplicate

Ask yourself the following four *Strategic Mindset* questions about each of the network-marketing skills listed above, and remember— if it can be taught, then you can learn it.

Strategic Mindset Questions

1. With this skill, do I have a clear strategy that I use and teach?

2. Can I point to and prove the effectiveness of that strategy?

3. Are the best practices in harmony with what my system teaches?

4. Do I know exactly how to help someone on my team break through what is holding them back from learning in this area?

Now, score yourself in the chart below on each of the seven skills from one to ten to see how strategic you are. You may want to go through this with one or more of the three people you listed previously with whom you have a connection in network marketing.

Instructions: In the boxes below each skill, rate yourself on a scale from one to ten, with ten being the highest, according to each question.	List	Appointments	Presentation	Product Information	Follow Up	Launch	Duplicate
Do I have a clear strategy that I use and teach?							
Can I point to and prove the effectiveness of that strategy?							
Are the best practices in harmony with what my system teaches?							
Do I know exactly how to help someone on my team break through what is holding them back from learning in this area?							

The seven network-marketing skills are really all you need to master and duplicate within your organization, as far as business-building skills. You can take your organization to a very high level with the right amount of activity in these areas, and yet there are thousands of people who will do them correctly without being really effective. So what's the issue? What's missing? If these skills are being properly developed and executed, then it usually boils down to one major piece that is missing.

The Effectiveness Skills

There are other skills that are primarily based on your character, which I call effectiveness skills, and you must have a *Strategic Mindset* around them. These are the skills that determine who really builds the massive organizations and reaches the highest levels. Focusing on and mastering these skills is what truly makes you a strategic networker.

Follow me on this... Sometimes when I (Ryan) am speaking with groups, I get a white board out and do this exercise with the crowd: I say, "When you have a large organization and you look out over your group and see leaders—you actually label people and say, 'This person's a leader and that person's a leader'—what causes you to say that about those particular people? What attributes do they have or what are they doing that would make you say they're a leader?" Here are the responses I typically get:

They have a great work ethic.

They are entrepreneurial.

They're competent in networking skills.

They're focused.

They're proactive.

They're trustworthy.

They are relational and have great people skills.

I list these attributes on the white board, and after I get about ten or fifteen I say, "Do we all agree, then, that if someone is doing these things, they're way more likely to build a massive business than someone who's not doing these things?" The whole crowd is usually in full agreement. Then I say, "Ladies and gentlemen, *this* is really the business. Yes, there are certain skills you have to have; you have to know how to build a list and make phone calls and schedule appointments. And yet all of that can be taught in one day. What makes some people succeed and others not, using the same exact system, are the attributes you've just listed. Having these characteristics is what *causes* people to make the phone calls and the presentations, to launch new members, and to be more effective than not. Talent and skill both matter; the good news is that everything you need to win in this business can be learned."

So you actually have to have both—the effectiveness skills and the business-building skills—and many people only have one or the other. Most of the effectiveness qualities can be developed as they learn how to work with people and understand personalities, and as they're plugged into the system of reading books, listening to audios and videos, and participating in events and conference calls. Leaders have to operate within that belief and accept the responsibility of teaching both sides of the equation.

The flip side of that coin is, as a leader you really shouldn't focus on people who just know how to do presentations. You should be looking to recruit people who already have the important qualities of a leader. What often happens is that people lower their standards and bring in people who have less influence, maybe because they think they are more easily sponsored or because they're broke and need money. There's nothing wrong with sponsoring someone who is broke. At twenty-five years old, I (Ryan) certainly didn't possess either the business-building skills or the effectiveness skills needed to build a massive organization. The first set of skills was easy to develop, though, once I accepted the "beliefs" mentioned in the previous section. I then just had to get out of my comfort zone for a while to practice. And yet it wasn't until I became aware of the need to grow in the area of effectiveness that I began to accelerate. Understand that I developed this awareness while I was still broke. And please understand that I didn't start making money first and then begin to grow personally. What really happened is that developing those skills became a *Strategic Mindset* that I started to embrace while I was building my business. In most cases, this awareness is all you need to break through to the next level. That "ah-ha" feeling you get is what uncovering a *Blind Spot* feels like. Now you just have to act on it.

Intentional Time Investment

Now that you're equipped with an understanding of the seven network-marketing skills and have a deep acceptance of how the effectiveness skills impact your results, let's talk about one of the hottest topics you'll deal with as a leader: *How do I spend my time?* The good news is, managing your time is also a skill, and that means you can learn how to do it. In reality, you can only invest your time into a small number of people, because you only have so much of it. Even if you have a group of 10,000 people, you're still going to be investing the bulk of your time with eight to ten; you just keep refining who those eight to ten are. You have to

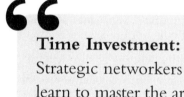

Time Investment: Strategic networkers learn to master the art of intentional time investment.

set standards and then teach the people in your organization what they have to do to access your time. This is what we refer to as intentional time investment, and it can be the difference between $50,000 a year and $1,000,000 a year. Yes, it's that powerful!

Intentional time investment is how Tony decides who he spends time with and who he is going to coach. He has a standard that he uses (called ADOME[2]) to evaluate potential clients to make sure the relationship would be a win for both of them. It doesn't mean,

---

2   A - Aggressive and appreciative, D – Desire to do business with us, O – Open-minded, M – Millions to be made, E – Equity play

though, that he isn't growing other people through his books and audios and videos; anything can be learned.

As strategic networkers, we should understand that the people who still need to grow their effectiveness qualities will not be on a fast track to build; it will be a few-year project for them. You can spend time with them, but do it in small bites and in a leveraged manner, and pay attention. Are they showing up for events? Are they plugging in to the calls? Are they attempting to make an effort?

When we set standards as strategic networkers, we can have our own form of ADOME. We simply must have a *Strategic Mindset* about who we are looking for and then intentionally invest our time seeking after and working with those people. If not, we will find ourselves chasing rabbits and not be any further along in our business five years from today than we are right now.

In reality, aren't we really wanting to spend our time with those who are developing and already have the effectiveness skills we listed above?

Let's look at them again, and this time from a time-investment mindset. Who would be the ideal, or PERFECT candidate to invest your time with? And understand, these mindsets are not necessary if you want to build a business—only if you want to build a *big* one.

The PERFECT Network Marketing Candidate

P   Proactive. You're looking to develop or find individuals who take initiative. If they don't, chances are this is not your person. You'll either want them to lead you to someone else or plug them into the system to grow.

E   Ethical (as in work ethic). If someone is lazy, this is not for them. If you feel you have to beg or plead with this person to build the business, *stop!*

R   Relational. People skills are the number-one skillset you're looking for. People who have them can either build a big business or lead you to those who can.

F   Focused. Does this person get distracted easily?

E   Entrepreneurial. It's a big plus to look for entrepreneurial-minded people. Trying to turn someone into a business owner who really wants to be an employee will wear you out!

C   Competent. Does this person grasp and model the seven strategic network-marketing skills? We're looking for those who can catch on quickly and follow directions. This is the only way they'll become competent in network marketing.

T   Trustworthy. If you can't trust them, don't work with them. It's that simple.

I (Ryan) will say that, for me, there's one thing that trumps all of these guidelines and gets my attention. If I see someone relentlessly trying, my heart is moved and I want to help them.

Using this as a guideline will effectively help you as a leader define who you want to recruit; but more importantly, it will show you who you should spend time with as your organization grows.

The bottom line is, you should be looking to intentionally invest time with those who are in alignment with your value system and are prepared to understand the proper way to think about skills. Now let's put the shoe on the other foot for a minute. If you can't honestly say that you are a PERFECT candidate for someone in your upline to spend time with, then it's time to make sure you become one. If you are, then it's time to learn the skill of intentionally investing your time the right way and with the right people.

Results

Strategy No. 3 VIP: We've all been getting the results we should be getting based upon two things: how we think, and what we do.

The reason you're reading this book is probably because you want better results. Let's face it—this is a results game. Either you're getting the results in business and in life that you want or you're not. Nothing else really matters, does it? No matter what happens to you or for you, if it yields undesirable results, you have a problem. In many cases, this is why Fortune 500 companies hire me (Tony). They simply want different results, and in order to get them they have to think about things differently than they did to get them where they are. This is also why we're writing this book, and why it is called *Becoming a Strategic Networker* and not *How to Build a Network Marketing Business*. There are plenty of books on how to build, and yet very few exist on how to think strategically about your network-marketing business.

We've talked throughout this chapter about how you can change your results by changing your mindset on beliefs and skills. I (Tony) want to show you how to think strategically at a whole new level that focuses on solutions rather than problems. The most successful people don't dwell on problems; they live in solutions. Today, change happens fast and often without warning, and it often leaves a string of problems in its wake. Yet change can also create opportunities to provide solutions to problems.

Strategic IQ

When we're attempting to produce optimal results, we're often inclined to develop a tactical response to a perceived problem. Here's an example: A typical network-marketing person's tactical approach to improving their sponsoring rate might be to sharpen their cold-calling script. That's pretty tactical. A better, more *strategic* approach might be to focus on learning about the prospect's challenges or dreams and communicating the solution as being a part of what you're offering. In network marketing, you're taught to discover and encourage your prospect's dreams. That's strategic! And yet you had to make the call and set the appointment in order to do that, which is tactical. Having that balance between thinking and doing is very powerful.

How about on the home front? Suppose you want your family to eat healthier food. A tactical approach might be to take a low-fat cooking class or get a new health-food cookbook, or even throw out all the junk food. These are wonderful approaches; however, how could you approach it more strategically? Maybe you could come up with a way to get your family to think more about nutrition. Strategic thinking often leads to long-term solutions rather short-term.

What's the difference between tactical and strategic? Tactical involves things like tasks, calls, activities, and paperwork. Strategic involves things like planning, thinking, and studying. In the last section, we talked about the business-building skills you need to develop, and most of those have to do with the tactical. If you focus only on those tactical activities, though, and don't operate from the more strategic effectiveness side and spend time planning, thinking, and studying, you won't build the massive organization you want to have. My late coach, friend, and former president Jim Norman once said to me, "Thinking is hard." He was talking about strategic thinking, and he knew few people did enough of it.

Just to stimulate your thinking, write down what percentage of the time you think you and/or your team operate in the tactical, and what percentage of the time you think you and/or your team operate in the strategic. Those two numbers should add up to 100 percent.

We've found that most people need to be more strategic.

> **Strategic IQ:** If you focus only on the business-building tactical activities and don't operate from the more strategic effectiveness side and spend time planning, thinking, and studying, you won't build the massive organization you want to have.

Howabout you? Was your tactical percentage pretty high? On the other hand we have found some who are too strategic. They plan, plan, plan, and then they plan some more. If that's you, you probably don't take enough action. As I go around the world, I find that about 90 percent of the people are so tactical that they're busy doing and doing and not strategically looking at all the pieces of the puzzle. I want to push you to think at that strategic level.

Strategic IQ is about balancing that out. A leader of a large network-marketing organization who is running a big event and is out setting up, running sound, and making sure the tool table is in place and that products are set out is an example of someone who is being too tactical. If this leader tells me (Ryan) that their income has grown stagnant and that they can't seem to find time to grow their business, my first round of counsel would be simple: If you want to develop a six- or even seven-figure income, you have to treat your business like a six- or seven-figure business. And a leader of that size business had better learn to leverage their time by developing a team, or they will never arrive. Often, letting go of the busy management side of growing an organization is the *Blind Spot* that is stumping all the results someone is looking for in their business. Since you're never going to make seven figures running

> **Best Use of Time:** Ask yourself this question often: *What's the best use of my time right now?*

sound at your events, why would you not want to develop someone else to do it? That example may be extreme; yet if you apply it to all the things that are sucking away your time, I'll promise you that it's affecting your results. The bottom line is, it's time to be more strategic.

Ask yourself this question often: *What's the best use of my time right now?* Sometimes the answer should be tactical, and sometimes it should be strategic. If you have an extra few minutes before or after a meeting, we encourage you to look at your list (hopefully you have your to-do list on your phone) to see what you have going on and ask yourself, *Do I need to be doing something tactical, like sending an email or following up on a call? Or do I need to lift up and look at my week or my month and see how things are going? Do I need to plan a weekend retreat with my top leaders?* People often miss this, and we want you to own it. Constantly ask yourself, *What's the best use of my time right now?*

As strategic network marketers, we all want better results. Our results come from our actions, our actions are dictated by our habits, and our habits are dictated by our thinking—or our *Strategic Mindset.*

With this in mind, I (Ryan) want to end this chapter with a couple of my teachings on how an incorrect mindset about time and goals could be messing with your and/or your team's results.

Here are some results robbers in disguise:

Time Invested versus Time Involved

Many people in this industry view time involved as an indicator of where their business should be. If they joined the company twelve months ago, they judge their results based on that length of time. It's not the length of time they've *been in* the business that matters; it's the time they've invested. It's entirely possible that they properly invested just ten to twelve hours during their year in business, and they *think* they've been working at it for a year. When they begin to shift their thinking over to *time invested versus time involved,* they tend to take on a new level of responsibility for their day-to-day action. They start asking the right questions about how they're spending their time, and they begin to view their *freedom* based on time invested versus time involved.

Strategy versus Goals

It's also important to understand the difference between strategy and goals. Most people in our industry learn to set goals, and they think that's the key to building their business. However, many of them never create a strategy to accomplish their goals. It's not enough to say you want to hit a certain rank or to even put a date on it. You must aggressively shift to strategy, which is the *action* plan designed to hit your goal in the time frame allotted. Designing a strategy should be based on tried and true concepts and developed with someone you respect and with whom you can create an accountability relationship (a peer you work well with).

Once you've designed a strategy, you're ready for the work. Before you start to execute the strategy, though, you have to make a decision: Will you accept full responsibility if the actions don't lead to the results you desire? Will you understand that if it doesn't happen, it's because of something you didn't do? Will you take on the *Strategic Mindset* that *all results create value* for a leader—even the bad ones? This mindset is important in network marketing, since most people (even leaders) quit this industry because of improper thinking toward their results. It wasn't too many years ago that my network-marketing business was taking off like a rocket. After five years of laying the foundation, we were finally reaping the rewards. Then it happened—one of my top leaders decided to get distracted with a new shiny object, and he joined another company. (Occasionally this happens.) He, of course, used his influence to recruit people he had a relationship with, and it resulted in an entire line of my business disappearing within a few months. Now this devastates some people, and yet real leaders in our industry learn from this and ask themselves the tough questions, like: *What could I have done better?* (There is always something you can do better). *What can I learn from this?* (There is always something you can learn). And *What can I do better going forward?* What weak leaders do is spend all of their time trying to attack the person who left instead of being proactive and working with the team that wants to stay. Remember, you learn from everything, and in the end you develop a calm form of leadership that real people want to be a part of.

At the end of the day, results in network marketing only change when the leader accepts responsibility for them. When you're willing to accept that responsibility, then you'll probably be willing to give it another shot, and eventually you'll hit your goals.

The bottom line is, if you want different results than what you are currently getting in your business, it's time to get rid of *Blind Spots,* and develop a more *Strategic Mindset*—a mindset that holds value in whom you spend time with while understanding that everything you need in this business is a skill; and if it's a skill, you can learn it.

In the next chapter, we'll explore the first step—Clarity—in my (Tony's) proven three-step *Strategic Acceleration* formula. Authentic vision has the power to pull you out of your circumstances and toward a better life and better results. This pulling power comes from having complete clarity about what you truly want. Clarity opens up new opportunities and connections and empowers you to better make strategic choices that will lead to superior results faster.

VIPs

☐ *Intentionally Strategic*: The very best top achievers, those who have extraordinary results in their life, are *Intentionally Strategic* in everything they do.

☐ Thinking: Almost every challenge you and your team will have is a mindset challenge.

☐ Beliefs: Your belief system ultimately determines the size of your income, the size of your team, and the impact you will have on others.

☐ *Blind Spots*: Learn to identify *Blind Spots* and correct beliefs that can hold you and your team back from reaching your potential.

☐ Real Leaders: Real leaders equip, empower, and encourage their team members to do the work. They first show them how to do it, then they do it with them, and then they let them do it on their own.

☐ Noise: The one thing that constantly challenges and undermines belief more than anything else is *noise*. Who you listen to matters!

☐ Skills: Strategic Network Marketers understand that their business is skill-driven; everything you need to be a top leader can be learned.

☐ Time Investment: Strategic networkers learn to master the art of intentional time investment.

☐ Results: We've all been getting the results we should be getting based upon two things: how we think, and what we do.

☐ *Strategic IQ*: If you focus only on the business-building tactical activities and don't operate from the more strategic effectiveness side and spend time planning, thinking, and studying, you won't build the massive organization you want to have.

☐ Best Use of Time: Ask yourself this question often: *What's the best use of my time right now?*

☐ Responsibility for Results: At the end of the day, results in network marketing only change when the leader accepts responsibility for them.

Self-Evaluation

On a scale of 1 to 5, with 5 being the highest, rate yourself on the six issues below to determine where you are in gaining a *Strategic Mindset* in your life and business.

1. I have examined my own beliefs and have sought input from mentors and family members to see if I have any *Blind Spots* that are keeping me from having the success I want in both my business and my personal life, including the four *Blind Spots* listed on pages 9 and 11.

2. I have a strong belief in my industry, in my company, in my products, in the opportunity this industry provides, and in myself. I often check for *Blind Spots* in each of these areas in myself, as well as in my team.

3. I have listed three people in my direct connections and three in my indirect connections that I will allow to speak into my life and influence my thinking, and I am allowing very few others, if any, to do so.

4. I have identified the skill sets I need to work on, both business and effectiveness skills, and I am seeking help from mentors/advisors and other personal development resources to grow in those areas.

5. I have determined my own *Strategic IQ,* as well as that of my team, and I am intentionally working to improve the balance between tactical and strategic in my business and life.

6. I accept personal responsibility for the results in my network-marketing business, as well as in my personal life.

Chapter Two

Clarity

One thing all successful network marketers have in common is that they are clear about where they're going. In contrast, many people reading this book are not. And outside of not having the proper *Strategic Mindset*, lack of clarity is the single biggest factor that is keeping you from reaching your potential.

I (Tony) have worked for many years with the top people at some of the most successful organizations in the world, across almost every industry, with over 1,000 clients to date—including dozens of network-marketing companies. I facilitate the level and speed of their success by helping them get clarity for themselves and their teams, get everyone really zeroed in and focused, and then execute well.

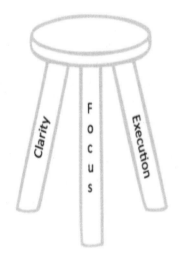

This proven formula—Clarity, Focus, and Execution—is the foundation of my life's methodology, set out in my best-selling book *Strategic Acceleration* (Perseus 2009). Those fundamental elements make up the three legs to the stool of success for any person or business. If one leg is missing, the stool will collapse and you most likely won't find the success you're reaching for.

Clarity is about understanding the vision—where you're going personally and/or professionally. On a scale of one to ten, how clear are you about where you're going with your network-marketing business?

On a scale of one to ten, with ten being the highest, my current *Clarity* score is: _____

Where am I going?

_____

_____

_____

_____

_____

How focused are you? Are you tied up with constant distractions, or are you focused every day on what matters most?

On a scale of one to ten, with ten being the highest, my current *Focus* score is: _____

What do I need to focus more on, and what distractions do I need to eliminate?

_____

_____

_____

_____

_____

How about execution? If you want results, you know you have to take action. You have to execute! Are you taking the action you should to become your very best?

On a scale of one to ten, with ten being the highest, my current *Execution* score is: _____

What actions do I need to take to execute well?

_____

_____

_____

_____

_____

In this chapter we dive into what it means to have clarity and how to get it. This is very strategic. Simply put, clarity doesn't happen by accident; it happens on purpose. We've identified three areas of your life that you can strategically develop on *purpose* to ensure ultra-clarity for your network-marketing business and for your life. This may be your breakthrough!

Clarity

Let's start out with some insight into clarity and its importance in network marketing. The basic definition of clarity is having an unfettered view of your vision—what you want—fed by an understanding of its purpose and value—why you want it. It's about developing a clear vision that aligns with your values, outlining priorities and objectives, and tackling goals with a real sense of urgency and focus. Clarity is achieved when you know where you are in relation to where you want to go. Knowing what you want actually creates a pulling power toward your vision.

Early in my networking career I (Ryan) lacked clarity about where I wanted to go and even why I would want to go there. Like most people, I signed up and witnessed the top earners walking the stage, traveling the world, leading big teams, and living the life of freedom. However, this didn't seem to motive me to do anything. What was missing was my clarity (my reason why). It wasn't until a few years later (in fact, two years after we had our first child) that clarity hit me. It was really simple: My wife was dropping off our two-year-old at day care each day, and then going to work. This was very upsetting for her; and at the end of each month, we were only adding about $1000 of income to our household. We finally realized that by making $1,000 a month in our network-marketing business, she could spend an extra 200 hours a month with our two-year–old child. At that point, this became a burning reason for me to develop a $1,000-a-month business. After all, our meetings (like yours) were filled with people who had done that, so to think we couldn't would have been a copout. It was simply a matter of whether we wanted it bad enough.

Here's another way of thinking about clarity and how it impacts your decision to build your business: Let's say there are two sky-scrapers that are 1,000 feet tall and 100 feet apart, with a four-inch-wide bridge connecting the two. Now let's say you are on top of one of the skyscrapers and someone on the other side says, "Come across the four-inch bridge and I'll pay you $1,000." Would you do it? My guess is that you wouldn't for $1000, for $5,000, or even for $100,000, since you know you would probably fall to your death.

Now let's rewind. Let's say the person on the other side of the four-inch bridge has kidnapped one of your children. They're holding your child up by their legs and they say, "If you don't come across this four-inch bridge in the next two minutes, I'll drop your child." My guess is that you would not hesitate one second. In that instance, your reason why (clarity) was so compelling and clear that you had to take action. You see, it's really not whether you can or you can't; it's whether your reason why (your clarity) is big enough to create a pulling power toward it.

To achieve clarity and take your business to the next level, you must answer this question for yourself: *What do I truly want from this business and why do I want it?* You have to be very clear at the outset to start succeeding, and even clearer to go to the highest levels. Often, the clearer you are, the higher the level of your results and the more likely you are to reach your vision.

Look at these four symptoms of poor clarity and assess how much they apply to where you are in your network-marketing business:

> **Poor Clarity Symptom Number One:** You don't believe you can do what you have to do. This is usually because you don't have clarity about what you truly want.

> **Poor Clarity Symptom Number Two:** You use planning to avoid taking action. Preparation and planning are important, and yet excessive preparation is nothing more than procrastination. Clarity destroys procrastination, because the action you need to take is vividly clear.

> **Poor Clarity Symptom Number Three:** You get stuck or resist leaving your comfort zone. Change isn't always easy; and unless you're willing to change, you will hang onto what's comfortable. Clarity inspires people to be willing to leave the familiar behind for something better.

> **Poor Clarity Symptom Number Four:** You quit or give up in the face of adversity or difficulty. Clarity of vision gives you the mental substance to persevere and overcome obstacle

If you're not clear about what you truly want, your belief in your effort will not be powerful or compelling enough to sustain your efforts. When you lack clarity, you will find yourself being pushed toward living in problems.

Without a clear vision, you're just traveling and rarely arriving. A clear vision pulls and energizes you toward getting what you want. We suggest you go as far as you can see in this fast-paced world, and then you can see farther. When you get more clarity as the weeks and months go by, you can make any tweaks or changes that are needed.

As a strategic networker, you can control three pieces to the clarity puzzle that, when properly aligned, bring clarity for you and for your team. I would argue that without these three things properly developed, you're doomed. The *big* three are:

> Values: The things that are most important to you and that guide your dreams (the "why")

> Dreams: Your aspirations, or the vision you have that inspires your goals (the "what")

> Goals: A set of intentional, strategic actions, with timelines, that lead to achieving your dreams (the "how")

If you want to be a higher achiever in the network-marketing business, you must have clarity in all three areas and ensure they are all three in alignment. Most people have *Blind Spots* about all three of these essential pieces for success—the need to identify their values, learning how to cultivate their dreams, and understanding how to effectively set goals. That's why we wrote this book—to help you uncover your *Blind Spots.* And once you've eliminated your *Blind Spots,* you can help others eliminate theirs.

> " **Clarity:** If you want to be a higher achiever in the network-marketing business, you must have clarity in three areas—your values, your dreams, and your goals—and ultimately all three must be in alignment. "

Strategic Networker Strategy No. 4

Values

Strategy No. 4 VIP: What you value should be the foundation for your goals, both personally and professionally.

When I (Ryan) was first getting started in personal development, I used a Franklin Planner—a personal development tool that has been used by many of the major success leaders, speakers, and executives over the years to organize and think about their lives. I knew that if I wanted to grow in leaps and bounds, I should observe and adopt the best practices, habits, and processes of successful people. And since I wanted to be even more productive than I already was, and I wanted to learn how to get the most out of every day of my life so I could reach my goals the fastest way possible, I decided to give it a try. (The planner, which started out in print format, has now evolved into an organizational tool that is available through various technology applications and smartphones.)

When I picked up my new organizational tool and began to read it, I discovered one question within its pages that caused me to stop and contemplate my life, my work day, and the way I'd been spending my time. That question was: *What do you value?*

Admittedly, it was the first time I'd ever thought about that question. Like most people, I was so busy doing and achieving that I hadn't really given my values much thought. But when I did, everything changed. When I made a list of the things I valued most, I was then able to center all of my daily actions on those things that were important to me.

A big part of clarity is having clearly defined values so you can make sure your goals align with the things you value most. British poet John Masefield wrote in his poem "Sea Fever," "All I ask is a tall ship and a star to steer her by."[3] Values are the stars that can help steer us to the results we truly want in our lives.

Many people make the mistake of jumping right into identifying their dreams and setting their goals instead of first clarifying their values. Most fail to take the time to step back before they create their action plan and say, *What is my life all about?*

I've since come to realize that most leaders, even those earning $50,000 or more a year, might not know what they really value. And because of this, they are in constant conflict; what they value is not in harmony with what they are shooting for, so there is an internal governor (for you car people) that won't let them go further, no matter how much potential they have. It is very frustrating!

If you want sustainable success, your action plan should include your values-based strategy. It's critical to establish clarity about what matters to you, what matters to your spouse, and what matters for your team. You don't want to create results and then find out they're the wrong results!

At one point years ago, I (Tony) had a beautiful setup of offices covering the world, and I was making powerful things happen and influencing millions of people. I remember specifically that I was in a hotel room in another country during that time, listening to an audio book by Billy Graham; and I heard something from this book that made a massive impact on me. In fact, it changed my life. In the book Dr. Graham poured out his heart to the readers, and one of the things I heard, in essence, was that he had put all of his energy into his ministry and failed at raising his kids. He couldn't take back that time and energy; he missed his opportunity to pour into his kids. I thought, *Here's a guy I and so many others greatly admire who truly missed out by not living in accordance with his values.*

---

3   John Masefield, "Sea Fever", Poetry Foundation, http://www.poetryfoundation.org/poems-and-poets/poems/detail/54932 (accessed 4/10/17).

What do you think that said to me? It said that I needed to change my business strategy and quit flying all over the world. I needed to be at home and be powerful for my kids. The results I wanted included much more than just money; I wanted my daughters to grow into incredible young adult women. So I closed my offices all over the world and built my *Success Acceleration Studio* right in my back yard on my estate, where top people fly in from all over the world to let me help them learn how to accelerate their results. And because I made the changes I needed to make, my wife and I have wonderful kids today who have very successfully launched out of the nest. I was getting extraordinary results before I made that change, and then I went to another level. I made my efforts more align with my values and can fortunately say that for over two decades since I made that change, both my business and my family have enjoyed a new level of success. Isn't that what you want—both personal and professional success?

Identifying values is an area that gets vastly overlooked in network marketing. Most people have a *Blind Spot* in this area and fail to take the time to be really clear on what their values are. There's an idea floating around in this industry that if people will just do the work we teach them to do, they'll hit their goals. We may teach them to build a dream of what they want to accomplish, and even to identify specific goals to make that dream a reality. Yet we fail to teach them to start with the most important step, which is to determine what they really care about—their values.

One of the things we've often talked about is why some succeed and others fail in this industry, using the same system. Obviously, not everyone gets the same results with the methods we teach. If you look across the leadership in a network-marketing organization, you'll discover that one of the differentiating factors is the unique ability to transfer dream and belief when they're communicating with their people. We believe the secret ingredient that gives some that ability is understanding the powerful connection between their values and their dreams and belief. That alignment is almost like a magnet that draws people to them. The clearer they are on their values as a leader, the more people are attracted to become part of their organization. Yes, there are people making millions of dollars in our industry who have never achieved that congruency; they've probably never even thought about intentionally aligning their dreams and belief with their values. However, because we know that making money is only part of the success puzzle, we're both convinced that most of those people are either unfulfilled or they're not living up to their potential.

> **"**
>
> **Dream and Belief:**
> One of the differentiating factors among leaders is the unique ability to transfer dream and belief when they're communicating with their people.
> **"**

When I (Ryan) sit down with leaders, I have credibility and they listen to me because my belief in what we're doing is so strong. Tony has that same credibility. He lives what he's teaching. And yet, even when someone meets Tony for the first time and hasn't had an opportunity to verify that, they can still *feel* that he is in alignment with something they want to be attached to. What they're feeling is that Tony is intentional about how his world works and fits together, which is something most people fail to deploy in both their personal life and in their business.

I'm sure you can identify leaders in your network-marketing business who are so clear on what they value and where they're going that people are attracted to them. Being a real leader in our industry involves more than just reading and repeating. You have to decide what you're going to accept as truth in your life so you stand a chance of being able to persuade a large organization. They may not all do what you say, but they will buy into you as someone worth following.

When I am communicating with a group of leaders, at least one of them will invariably say to me, "I have people who have done fifty meetings and have either signed a few people who haven't duplicated or haven't had anyone join their organization." Those people are going through the motions; and yet they're not transferring belief, because they've not yet identified what they value in life and connected it to the network-marketing vehicle. Until that piece comes together, it just doesn't seem to happen. People are joining you, as much as or more than they are deciding whether to be in business with your company. If you have two people presenting their business to a prospect using the exact same words, and one has made this connection in his own life and one has not, the person who has is much more likely to get the prospect to believe in what they're saying and see how the business would benefit them. When you bring a new person into your organization with whom you're going to invest time, make sure they have an understanding of what they value so they can make that connection.

> **Do this now:** As a leader, step back and assess whether you are really clear on your own values as you're clarifying your dreams and goals.

Your Top 10

Do this now. We encourage you, as a leader, to step back and assess whether you are really clear on your own values as you're clarifying your dreams and goals. We've included in the Appendix a list of sixty major values (of course, you may add more if you don't see some of your values listed). Use this list to conduct what I (Tony) call a "values clarification tournament." First, go through and mark the twenty values that are most important to you. Then go through and identify the top ten of those twenty, in no particular order of priority, so you end up with the ten things that you value most. Write your top ten in the spaces below and snap a picture with your phone. Save it as your lock screen photo and review it whenever you can. Then help the people in your organization do the same. Do this same exercise with those in your inner circle, with any new people you bring in to your organization, and even with your spouse and your kids, so you're really supporting their wins.

My Top Ten Values:

1. _____
2. _____
3. _____
4. _____
5. _____
6. _____
7. _____
8. _____
9. _____
10. _____

Obviously, the fastest way to build a network-marketing business is to find people who already know their why because they have identified and are living their values. However, if you want to build a sustainable, long-term income, you must develop a team culture that supports the development of this principle.

Here are some common misalignments between goals and values:

1. Your primary goal is to reach a certain level in your company, and your primary value is spending time with your children. If you don't think through your goal and find a way to properly support your value, you will constantly

be a playing a mind game. Many people start out saying, "I'm going to build my network-marketing business so I can spend more time with my family." Then ten years go by, and while they're out trying to build a business that will enable them to spend time with their family, they miss a whole decade-long window of doing just that. They've sold themselves on the idea that building their business is actually going to cause them to be out of alignment with their value. The reality is, you can do both. We believe you can get to the highest level in this industry and not have regrets.

Let me (Ryan) give you an example. I recently held a large event for my organization, and I took my son with me. I spent a lot of time with my team, and yet I also spent a lot of extra time with my son, just hanging out in the hotel room and having fun. I gave him a job to do (videoing parts of the event) and he felt important. He was excited to go, and afterwards he was glad he went. He didn't get to hang out with anyone his age the entire weekend, and yet he had a blast. There are so many wins in this scenario, and all it requires is a decision to be intentional about aligning your values with your dreams and goals.

Remember Tony's story about closing his offices all over the world and building a studio in his back yard on his estate so he could be home with his family? He found a way to build an extremely successful business and still be present and connected with his family. His game plan was to be there for twenty years raising his kids, and then once the kids were raised, to move back to corporate life. His kids are now successfully launched out of the nest, and he's building a new RESULTS Center that will allow him to serve his clients on a whole new level. All of that was intentional, long-term, strategic thinking that was connected to his values, dreams, and goals.

2. Your goal is personal development, and yet you don't have a value that matches that. You don't take the time to read the books, listen to the audios, and watch the videos that cause you to grow. We both voraciously devour those tools every day, because we know we can't grow as a person or grow our businesses if we don't value personal development to the extreme. It's very common in our industry for a leader to preach personal development; and yet because they've arrived at a certain level, they no longer have the focused action to keep growing themselves. When they do that, they cap themselves on what they can actually deliver to their organization.

3. Your goal is a six-figure income and your value is freedom. First, recognize that a six-figure income does not make you free unless your lifestyle is in check. (Remember Tony's example.) If your value is freedom, you need to figure out what it takes for you to be free, and that should be your goal. If you're focused on anything other than what's going to tie your goal to your value, you're probably just chasing something for the sake of chasing it, and it will likely not happen.

Here's another extremely important point to the values issue: In order to succeed at the very top level in this industry, you must make sure your values align with the corporate values of the company you work for, or find a company whose values do align with yours. In our industry, many people get so focused on building their own brand that they sometimes create a conflict with the corporate brand. There's certainly nothing wrong with branding yourself; and yet if you're not in alignment with the company's brand, you'll be creating dysfunction in your group while you're doing it, and your organization won't grow. Make sure there's *Intentional Congruence* between your values and the company's values and guidelines.

Let me (Ryan) share with you something that is a constant value conflict in our industry. Often, as you're growing your team, some very talented, influential people will show up in your organization who either don't nec-essarily share your value system or don't match the network-marketing industry to their values. So what usually hap-pens is that leaders end up spending all their time and energy trying to get these people to change their value sys-tem, and in the process it burns out both the leader (you) and the person they're trying to change. The truth is, you have to learn when

> **Alignment with Corporate Values:** In order to succeed at the very top level in this industry, you must make sure your values align with the corporate values of the company you work for, or find a company whose values do align with yours.

to back off so you don't burn the relationship. They just may not be ready; and if you wear them out, they'll never want to be in business with you. The best thing you can do is move in a new di-rection and build with some new people and with new energy. Too often, leaders try to force people to become something they're not, or at least that they're not ready for. That destroys their relationship, so they never stand a chance of having those people come around six months, a year, or even five years down the road.

I've had people join my organization five or more years after I originally spoke with them, because the timing was not right in the beginning. I handled the relationship correctly; and now that some of their values have shifted and they've made some adjust-ments in their lives, and our industry is more in alignment with their beliefs, they've decided to join. They were just not ready years ago, and I could have easily burned that relationship.

On the flip side of that, I have a lot of talented people in my organization who aren't doing anything. Here's the *Strategic Mindset* way of thinking about that: If I maintain the right kind of relationship and contact with those people, they will be a tremendous reservoir for my future. I've seen so many leaders wear out everyone they come in contact with, to the point that they no longer have any influence with them, and they lose that asset. Even during my long relationship with Tony, there have been occasions when the timing was off on certain things, and I had to get some things more in alignment before it would work. During those times, Tony was patient and maintained a great relationship with me, and it paid off for him and me in the end. (As you can see, we don't advocate the MLM junkie approach of viewing people as a way to riches. Instead, we support the strategic-networking approach, which values relationships and, as such, is embodied with long-term thinking.)

The network-marketing industry literally revolves around the value of relationships. And although we don't like to tell anyone what their values should be, we have both observed that this is the *top* most common value among all strategic networkers. You don't necessarily have to value relationships to make money; however, you do have to value them to successfully lead a team. And the fact that you picked up this book lets us know that you want to strategically lead a team.

If you believe you have not valued relationships properly up to this point, the good news is that you can decide to grow and learn in this area. As a matter of fact, I (Tony) wrote a book a while back to help people with this, called *Rich Relationships, Rich Lives: It's All about the Win-Win*. Strong relationships (especially in the network-marketing industry) help you leverage your career growth, expand your success, create your legacy (both personally and professionally), and live a happier, more powerful and influential life.

I've also helped make popular the term *Relationship Capital,* which is the payback you get from the time, effort, and rapport you've invested in building and nourishing relationships, whether they're with family, friends, or business colleagues and clients. You could say that by the time you've reached the mastery level outlined in this book, you have so much *Relationship Capital* that your success will be perpetual for the rest of your life, provided you maintain your value system.

To get the most out of the relationships in your network-marketing business, you need to be strategic, intentional, and disciplined. By "strategic" I don't mean "manipulative." In fact, being strategic about your relationships means creating win-wins that will set you up with a better chance for achieving what you want from each of them. Being intentional involves scheduling time with each of the relationships that are important to you, knowing what's important to them, and ensuring you feed those things. Let people know they have value to you. They will begin to notice that they are important to you and will want to reciprocate. Being disciplined is the equivalent of living good habits—like building, nourishing, and fostering positive relationships.

Here are a couple of other tips about relationships. Be sure and share these with the leaders in your organization. We believe that the values attached to these are vital to a strategic networker:

1. Surround yourself with successful, positive people.

   ☐ Some people can be toxic to your emotions, energy, and motivation.

   ☐ Some people can be motivating and inspiring, and they literally give you energy. You want to be intentional about who you surround yourself with. (We'll talk more about this later.)

   ☐ List the people you want to spend time with.

   ☐ Write down what people care about, and then see how you can feed that.

2. Saying "No"

- ☐ When and why should you say no? To save time, when someone pulls your energy down, and when people don't ever become self-sufficient.
- ☐ "No" doesn't have to be a complete no.
- ☐ Understand that it's not always rude to say no, especially if you give them an alternative or the reason.
- ☐ Use the word "because" to trigger you to give people the why.

As a leader, no matter how much or how little you're making in this business, if you will address this issue about relationships early on, you'll have a long career in the network-marketing industry. If you don't, you'll make a little bit of money and that will be it.

You've now identified your top values to give you clarity as to what your life is all about (your purpose), and you understand the importance of aligning your dreams and goals with those values. Now let's talk about the strategy of maximizing the dream so you'll have further clarity—a roadmap, in fact, that will help you close the gap between where you are now and where you want to be.

Dreams

Strategy No. 5 VIP: Putting actions to your dreams and influencing others to do the same is like adding rocket fuel to your business engine.

Dreamers are attractive. Let's face it, we're all fascinated by stories of Walt Disney, Henry Ford, and Steve Jobs. I (Ryan) think we're all motivated by the big dreamers in the world; and yet if we're not careful, we can overwhelm the people just starting out in this business by projecting the idea that they, too, must have larger-than-life dreams if they ever want to succeed in network marketing. We have to help them start where they are. What would be a small dream to us may be a huge dream to them; it could be just as motivating for them to dream of making a hundred thousand dollars a year as it would be for me to dream of making a million dollars a year, and we have to keep that in perspective.

Merriam-Webster defines "dream" (in the context we use it here) as "a strongly desired goal or purpose." Its next definition, though, is "something that fully satisfies a wish."[4] Your dream may start out as simply a wish, with no commitment to action. In fact, your wishes can go anywhere you want, with no measure of reality attached. You can wish you lived on the moon, or even that you could be a top earner in your business tomorrow. Or your wish may actually have the promise of becoming a dream if you were willing to put feet to it. When your wish moves into the realm of

---

4   Merriamwebster.com, s.v. "dream."

a dream, it begins to line up with the possibility of reality. Have you ever found yourself saying, "Just maybe…"? When you start to attach actual potential to a dream and can see the real possibility of fulfilling it with the right kind of action, that's when the adrenaline kicks in and it becomes a "strongly desired goal or purpose."

Dreams are what make network marketing such a great industry; and yet at the same time, dreams are also what give our industry a bad name. It's not that the word "dreams" is a problem; it's because so many people in this business never have their dreams fulfilled. The missing element here is that they don't properly attach goals, or strategy, to their dreams to make them a reality. We almost make it sound like if they just dream big enough and get out and do certain things, it will happen. The truth is, they could actually achieve a lot of those dreams if they set realistic goals and develop a strategy—a specific action plan—for achieving them. It's okay to get excited about owning a yacht, and yet that yacht doesn't materialize without having a goal and a strategy to get it. Dreams without goals will virtually never be realized, and goals without strategies will seldom see real results.

> **Dreams to Goals to Strategies:** "Dreams without goals will virtually never be realized, and goals without strategies will seldom see real results."
> —Ryan Chamberlin

The number one skill a network marketer can have is to learn how to sell a dream. Because this is so powerful, we believe that dreaming and helping others dream should also be viewed as a strategy. Understand that there's much more to it than just hype. When people finally identify what they're dreaming of, the two things that will almost always determine whether they can accomplish their dream will be time and money. When someone has a burning desire to accomplish their dream and they see network marketing as the vehicle to help them do that, you have a win-win. The strategy isn't just to get people dreaming; it's to get them dreaming the right way so they match up the network-marketing vehicle with the solution. And please understand that this strategy must never cross over into manipulation; for if it does, it will be out of alignment with your values. It *must* be authentic.

The best way to cultivate a dream is through the stories of the people who have fulfilled their dreams. That's why conventions and testimonial audios and videos are such powerful strategies to instill the dream into your team. More often than not, we don't come up with dreams on our own. We usually get inspired about something when someone paints a picture of it through their story. That's what happened in my life; someone inspired me to think bigger than I was thinking in some areas, and that turned into a dream.

Creating a Dream Plan

In network marketing, we want people to dream *big;* and since we'll be helping them turn those dreams into goals so they can become a reality, we want them to start with the end in mind. We want them to dream big in the areas of life that are ultimately in harmony with their values system, and they can do that by understanding the balance wheel of life.

The Balance Wheel of Life

In my book *Designing Your Own Life,* I (Tony) talk about the balance wheel of life. It's not about having perfect balance. The ultimate goal is having a constant focus, *being aware*, and *being intentional* about achieving balance in the six areas of life. For instance, in our early twenties we are sometimes more focused on education, on home life in our thirties, and so on. What we want to encourage is managing balance in six vital areas:

"
Balance Wheel of Life:
In the balance wheel of life,
it's not about having perfect
balance. The ultimate goal is
having a constant focus, being
aware, and being intentional
about achieving balance in
the six areas of life.
"

1. **Financial/Business:** Financial dreams can translate into many things: peace of mind, the ability to donate to charitable causes, security for your children, pleasure, etc. This is also where your network-marketing goals go. Balance in this area could include hitting a certain pin level or volume in your business without sacrificing time with your family.

2. **Physical/Health:** Your health and fitness are extremely important to having a satisfying, productive life. Dream big. What do you want to look like or be able to do that you currently can't do?

3. **Home and Family Life:** An atmosphere of faithfulness and commitment will ensure that your family thrives. Balance in this area includes investing time with your family. Dreams of having fun together, going on family vacations, or purchasing jet skis fit perfectly here.

4. **Educational:** Continual learning is crucial to having a balanced life. Educational dreams can include formal (university) or informal (personal development through reading, listening, and staying current on world issues).

5. **Social:** A healthy, balanced life has a social aspect that brings happiness. This could include travel, as well as relationships and social interactions with friends and colleagues.

6. **Spiritual:** Spiritual balance, which includes both serving and worship, helps guide and gives direction.

Ask yourself, *What is the optimal scenario for me in each of these areas of my life? What would make me so excited in each area that I could hardly stand it if it were not to happen for me?*

Please understand that any dream can be valuable. It's been proven, however, that when goals are properly set (which we'll go over in the next section) and achieved in these six areas, you'll be more fulfilled. And since goals begin with *dreams,* it's important to begin *dreaming* big in the six areas of the balance wheel of life.

Before we ask you to identify your dreams in these six areas, let me (Tony) say that I believe most people in this business are too singular in the area of dreams. They link them only to the things they want to have: I want to *have this house,* I *want to have this car,* and *I want to have this bank account.* What you want to have is just one piece of the puzzle if you really want to live at the mastery level we talked about in chapter one. Three other important pieces to consider are what you want to share, experience, and give. The fifth piece—and perhaps the most powerful—is who you want to become. Most people fail to even have this piece on their awareness window.

> **Who You Become:** If you want to be stable, exceptional, and ongoing in this business, we believe that who you become should be a huge part of your dreams and goals.

Have you thought through your dreams with this kind of clarity? Unless you have, you simply won't be as clear as you need to be to maximize your life and business potential. *If you want to be stable, exceptional, and ongoing in this business, we believe that who you become should be a huge part of your dreams and goals.*

Now that you've examined your dreams in light of what you want to have, share, experience, give, and become, write down your *ultimate* dreams in these six areas now:

Your Financial/Business DREAMS

_____

_____

_____

_____

_____

_____

Physical / Health DREAMS

_____

_____

_____

_____

_____

Home and Family Life DREAMS

_____

_____

_____

_____

_____

Educational DREAMS

_____

_____

_____

_____

_____

_____

Social DREAMS

_____

_____

_____

_____

_____

_____

Spiritual DREAMS

_____

_____

_____

_____

_____

_____

Visualization

If you want to be a strategic network marketer, you'll ultimately need to learn how to effectively turn these dreams into proper goals. This begins with visualization. Realize that outstanding athletes and CEO's do this, and we know for a fact that strategic networkers do it, as well. How does that work?

Have you ever decided you want to buy a certain car, and then you suddenly started "seeing" that particular make and model car everywhere? Those cars had been there all along; it's just that your reticular activating system, or RAS, had suddenly kicked in to make you notice them, since it knew that was something you were interested in.

Scientifically speaking, the RAS is a set of nerves at the bottom of your brain that allows you to bring things into your brain that you need, want, or desire. Its function is to act like a sorting office, evaluating the incoming information (from all senses) and prioritizing what gets into your brain, and eventually what gets your attention. Because your conscious brain can't capture everything, the more serious you are about what you want and focus on, the more your subconscious focuses to achieve it. In fact, your conscious mind can consume 40 bits of data per second, while your subconscious mind can consume 40 million bits of data per second. That's powerful. If you have a dream that you've turned into a goal, then, your RAS knows that's something you're really interested in, and it allows it to come into your brain.

When you understand that writing down and visualizing your dreams turns them into goals and activates your RAS, you can strategically use the power of your brain to help you reach your goals. In reality, most people don't set goals because they lack an understanding of the RAS.

Since the reticular activating system filters things you've dreamed about and written down as goals to come more often into your line of focus, they then become part of the law of attraction, and that has a huge impact on helping you achieve those goals. You not only see the goals in your mind; you also begin to see things around you that will help you achieve your goals. If you don't write your dreams down, then your brain likely does not recognize them as goals and is not as clear about their importance; therefore your RAS may filter out things you might need to help you achieve them.

Let me (Tony) give you three keys to leveraging your RAS and making your dreams a reality:

1. Write down with clarity what you really want.

2. Visualize it.

3. Use congruent self-talk to help you achieve your dreams and goals.

Results Boarding: Using the RAS to Get More of What You Want

High achievers are extremely clear about what they want, and they turn their dreams into goals and then visualize their goals to keep them in crystal-clear focus. If you've been in the network-marketing industry for any length of time, you've probably heard of a dream board or vision board. And now that you understand the scientific basis of the RAS and how utilizing it properly can help you achieve better results in your life, we invite you to think of this practice from here on out as "results boarding." Results boarding is a very powerful tool that actually triggers your RAS, because it's a visual representation of the results you want to achieve in your life. And if you're wondering whether this is a legitimate business strategy for any industry, understand that this is the exact same method that I teach to my Fortune 400-500 clients when they want to take their life to the next level.

To get started, go to a store like Home Depot or Lowes and buy a stack of one-foot-square cork boards (they usually come in sets of thirty-two). Decide where you want to put your results board so you can see it every day, and then just start putting up the squares. You can make it any size you want—anywhere from one square to four by four, or even four by eight if you want a big one. You can add to it as your dreams grow.

After you have the cork board up, put a sign at the top that says "Results Board." Then put pictures on the board of anyone who will be involved in achieving your dreams and goals—if you're doing this for your team, put a picture of your team on there; if you're doing it for yourself, post a picture of yourself; and if it's a family vision board, put a picture of your family on there.

One of the powerful things that people often miss is having a family mission statement. I encourage you to create one, and then put your family mission statement right in the center of your results board if you have a family, or your personal mission statement if you don't. Then I encourage you to post a list of the values you just identified, because you want everything you visualize to be congruent with your values. Then start collecting pictures that represent your dreams, pulling from magazines, your personal or family picture albums, or items you see on the computer, and post them. Build your results board out and look at it over and over and over again. And if you have a family, I encourage you to get your family involved in building your results board so you're all seeing it all the time.

Building a results board is a powerful concept, and it really does work. Here's a picture of mine:

Throughout your network-marketing career, your results board will continue to fuel your dreams, and your dreams will continue to fuel your goals.

Congruent Self-Talk

The third key for leveraging your RAS is something many of people miss, and I don't want you to miss it: positive self-talk that is congruent with your goals. For example, if your goal is to be organized and you say things like, "Well, you know, I am not a very organized person," then you have self-sabotaged. You need to be saying positive things like, "I'm getting more organized so I can reach my goals."

So now, with your dreams written down, your results board in motion, and your self-talk positively aligned with your goals, you're ready to develop your written goals plan. Let's dive into how you can turn those dreams into written goals and obtain clarity for you and your team like never before.

Goals

Strategy No. 6 VIP: Your network-marketing goals should add value to all areas of your life.

Goals are simply dreams with a strategic action plan attached to bring them to reality. And as such, goals go even further than dreams in helping your RAS filter out things that don't matter and focus on the things that are important to you. They allow the right things to come into your mind, and hence your life, intentionally. They allow you to get clearer on where you are today and where you want to go, focus on the right things to help achieve your targets, and help you execute for results. Goals give you a blueprint, or a map, for designing your best life.

Before we get into how to set goals, it's important to understand that your network-marketing business will be layered on top of all six areas of the balance wheel of life. Network marketing is not the only solution to help you achieve the dreams you documented, of course, and yet it is certainly one of the most extremely viable solutions. Consider this: The right amount of money and/ or the right amount of time could have an impact on helping you achieve virtually every goal you have. Right? Since money and time are a big part of your goals, what would happen if you were earning more money, were passionate about what you're doing, and were working less hours than you've ever worked? This is really the power behind the network-marketing vehicle. It's actually a goal-achieving machine, especially considering that most people currently don't have a solution for achieving the dreams and goals they're focused on. When they become strategic about their net-work-marketing business, this can all change.

What's Your Number?

We mentioned in chapter one a question I (Ryan) ask often when I'm speaking or working with my team: What's your number? In most cases, there's a certain dollar amount that would enhance each of the six areas in your balance wheel of life if it were coming in to your household on a monthly basis in a residual format (you knew it was coming, no matter how many hours a week you worked). It may be $1,000 a month, or it may be $50,000 a month, or somewhere in between. (And guess what? Every member of your team has a number too!) Whatever the number, it would certainly help you fulfill your health goals, because it would relieve the stress of your financial burden. In fact, if you could figure out how to get relief in the area of finances, it would support not only your health goals, but also your goals that relate to travel, more family time, donations to your church or other charities, and almost all of your other goals. If you met all of your health goals, all of your social goals, or all of your educational goals, none of them would improve almost every other area of your life like meeting your financial goals would.

Once you really understand the power of what the income from your network-marketing business can do for you, you'll want to be more strategic and determine how to get from Point A to Point B as quickly as possible. You won't want it to take fifteen years. It really is a one- to two-year project, in most cases, to get to an income stream that would fuel relief and enjoyment in all six areas of your life.

How to Set Goals

I (Ryan) want to share with you a goal-setting exercise that I've been teaching the last few years that has helped hundreds—maybe thousands—learn how to set goals in a more powerful way. You'll notice that we've incorporated the six areas of the balance wheel of life. This method is something you can begin using right now with your teams as individuals or groups, and even at massive events. Goal-setting is something that most people hear their entire life that they should do, and yet very few actually do it.

I developed this teaching from information I gleaned from three great sources: (1) value concepts and clarity ideas from Tony Jeary, (2) a goal-setting seminar presented by Jim Rohn, which basically changed the way I thought about goal-setting, and (3) a book called *The Power of Focus*, by Jack Canfield, Mark Victor Hansen, and Les Hewitt,[5] which changed the way I thought about balancing my goals. I designed it as a fifteen-minute workshop to help people quickly expand their thinking about the goal-setting process, which will benefit them throughout their lifetime.

When I'm teaching this material in live events, I hand out worksheets for the participants to use. Since you don't have access to the worksheets, a simple legal pad will do.

Goal-Setting, Part One

Part one of our goal-setting exercise is a set of six questions that are designed to get your brain spinning and your dream wheel rolling. As you go through the questions, I want to encourage you to write down the first answer that comes to your mind, because studies have shown that what you write down in the first thirty seconds is really what's on your mind. Here are the questions:

1. In thirty seconds or less, write down the three most important goals in your life right now.

2. If someone handed you a million dollars, tax-free, and they said at the end of the next thirty days they would take back what you hadn't spent, what would you do with it?

---

5   Some information in this section was taken from *The Power of Focus*, by Jack Canfield, Mark Victor Hansen, and Les Hewitt (Health Communications, Deerfield Beach, FL, 2000).

3. What would you do if you went to the doctor, and he said, "You're going to be healthy for the next six months, but at the end of that time you will die"?

4. What have you always wanted to do but held back from doing it because of your finances, your job, or your situation? In other words, what would you do if time and money were no object?

5. What type of activities are you really passionate about doing that give you the greatest feelings of importance?

6. If you were granted one wish to do anything, and you were guaranteed that you could not fail, what would it be?

Goal-Setting, Part Two

Are you ready to get serious about writing some goals? Leaving a wide left margin, write down forty (or more) things that come to your mind that you want to accomplish, pulling from the dreams you wrote down in the balance wheel of life. It could be: *I want to support a certain charity. I want to buy a certain vehicle. I want to pay off a certain credit card. I want to take a certain trip with the family. I want to improve my parenting skills so I can become a better parent.* [Note: At this point, these are still dreams; by the time we complete the exercise, however, they will be goals, because we'll attach strategic actions that will make the dreams a reality.] Take the time to write down the goals that are coming to your mind right now. Have fun with it! You can do this with your family, with your spouse, and with your children. We do it with our four boys, and we have a blast.

Goal-Setting, Part Three

In part three, you're going to go back and detail out your list. Here's where you really turn your dreams into goals. In a portion of the left margin next to every goal, put a "T" (which stands for "Time) and write down the number 1, 3, or 5, depending on whether you want to accomplish that particular goal in the next year (1), three years (3), or five years or *more* (5).

Goal-Setting, Part Four

Part four is one of my favorites, because that's where we categorize our goals. In the Dreams section of this chapter, we talked about the six categories in the balance wheel of life. Go back to pages 60 and 61 and review the descriptions of those six areas; and then, also in the left margin, go through and categorize the forty goals you've written down. Write the letter "C" (for category) beside each goal, and then write down the letter(s) that coincides with those categories:

1. "F" for Financial/Business
2. "P" for Physical/Health
3. "H" for Home and Family Life
4. "E" for Educational
5. "So" for Social
6. "S" for Spiritual

Goal-Setting, Part Five

Now that you've gone through and answered the six questions that got your mind thinking about the dreams and goals that are important to you, you've written a list of at least forty goals, you've put time frames on them, and you've categorized your goals, the next part of the exercise is where you really realize the power of goal-setting. This part will reveal several things to you and will help you take your goal-setting to the next level.

Go to a blank page of your legal pad, and label it "Prioritizing." Then, out of the goals you listed, put down the three most important one-year goals, the three most important three-year goals, and the three most important five-year-or-longer-goals that you listed. When you transfer them over to this sheet so you can see them, you're going to get excited, because you'll begin to realize that the network-marketing vehicle you've chosen is going to allow you to have both time and money to allow you to enjoy the realization of these goals.

In this part, you may come to the realization that you're heavy in one-year goals and yet don't have enough three- and five-year goals. Or you may be heavy in five-year goals and not have enough in one-year goals. This will be a very revealing part of the process for you, and it's important to go back and begin to think through time frames and make sure you have enough goals for each. The purpose of this exercise is not just to have goals for each time period, but for you to be able to really identify where you want to go in life (have clarity), and ultimately to make sure that you have believable and achievable short-term goals that lead you to the long-term results you desire. You'll also want to make sure that your results board reflects your short- and long-term goals.

Goal-Setting, Part Six

Now let's go back and see how you can manage the balance wheel of your life. Tony and I both are convinced that people can make a lot of money, and yet that doesn't mean they're happy. They may even have great relationships and still not be happy, because they haven't managed balance in their lives.

To begin this process, all you need to do is tally the letters on a separate sheet of paper. How many of those forty goals are financial/business goals? How many are social goals, spiritual goals, health goals, home and family life goals, or educational goals? If thirty-three out of forty are financial/business goals, you may run into some problems with your family, with your church, or with your relationships. You may not be planning vacations with your family, and you'll get burned out. If you have thirty-three relationship goals, you may have some great relationships, and yet you're going to be broke. You won't be able to do anything with them. You'll feel out of balance and frustrated. When you decide to dedicate a portion of your time to accomplishing one significant goal in each of these six areas over the next sixty days, you will start enjoying what most people are desperately striving for, and that's more balance. Remember, the ultimate goal is *having a constant focus*, *being aware*, and *being intentional* about achieving balance. When you have enough one-year, three-year, and five-year (or more) goals, and enough spread over the six categories, you'll be happier and more fulfilled.

Goal-Setting, Part Seven

So what's your balance wheel of life? Taking the information you've written so far, document on a separate sheet the *top five goals* you want to focus on in each area within the next twelve months, as well as some key words that resonate the most with the goal. For example, if your goal is to take a vacation with your family, your key words may be "family intimacy." Then do the same exercise for three-year and five-year goals.

The final step for turning your dreams into goals is to make an action plan to move each goal forward. This book is full of strategies that will give you direction as you consider what action steps to take. Do that now. On a clean sheet of paper, write down each of the goals you identified in this last step, and list under each goal at least three action steps you can take to make that goal a reality. Now, execute your plan!

Now that you've completed the entire exercise, you have a great first draft of your life goals, and you probably have much more clarity than you've ever had.

As a strategic networker, the most important thing you can do is to look at your business as the vehicle that will help you achieve the goals you've listed in each of the six areas of the balance wheel of life. Understanding that is what will motivate you and the leaders on your team more than anything else.

I've identified below some specific goals that will drive your network-marketing business. These goals are separate from and in addition to the goals you've identified for the six areas of your life.

Specific Network-Marketing Goals and Phases

Understand that these goals should generally be included in all phases of your network-marketing business. I have identified them out of literally thousands of conversations and coaching sessions that keep coming back to these topics. I believe that someone who is going to be strategic in their network-marketing business will not only set these as weekly, monthly, quarterly, annual, three-year, and five-year goals, but they will also coach their team to do the same.

Here are the five goals and the key words that describe the biggest benefit of each:

1. Personal and team sponsoring goals (excitement and belief)

2. Personal and team presentation goals (momentum)

3. Personal income goals (lifestyle)

4. Number of participants at local, regional, and national events goals (team development)

5. Personal and team rank and promo goals (recognition)

In my experience, you'll never stop needing to focus on these five goals. Your effectiveness skills, as taught in chapter one, will have an impact on your results in these areas. And although these five goals will be part of your goal-setting throughout your career, what can change drastically are the strategies used to reach the goals.

These strategies are usually determined by which phase you're in as a strategic networker. And in each of the phases outlined below, you'll see how these five network-marketing goals interact.

Strategic Approach: How you approach goal-setting in the four phases of your business will determine your daily focus and thus your ability to ultimately achieve your goals.

The key is to identify which phase you and your team members are in, and set your business goals accordingly.

I (Ryan) believe there are actually four phases of goal-setting in the network-marketing industry, and these phases determine your approach. The phases are: short-term, mid-term, long-term, and legacy goals. How you approach goal-setting in the four phases of your business will determine your daily focus and thus your ability to ultimately execute your goals. And although every company has a different compensation plan, if your goal is to be a six-figure earner within this industry, there is a common way of thinking about your approach. Let's break those down:

Strategic Approach to the Four Phases of Network Marketing Goal-Setting

Phase One: Short Term Goals—One to Three Months (The Foundation for Momentum)

There's a strategic way to teach new people in this industry how to think as they kick off their business. If they will start out with a ninety-day run, where they block out everything and go full speed ahead, they'll have an excellent chance of developing a six-figure income within twelve to twenty-four months. And no matter where you are in your network-marketing organization or how long you've been there, ninety days of massive action and the *right activity* will create the *foundation for momentum.*

Your goals for that ninety-day period will need to focus on building your business. Your life will actually be out of balance for that brief period, because you'll be in the process of launching something and will need to put extra energy into it. There will be more calls, more meetings, more of everything. That will produce the foundation so you can then go into the run-up to your first year.

The reality is, as a leader, there will be several times throughout your career that you will either need to go on a ninety-day run yourself or lead your team to do one. One ninety-day run may help you to establish your business; however, it obviously won't take you to a seven-figure income. Your goals—or the expansion of your goals—will determine how many

> **66**
>
> **Ninety-Day Run:** No matter where you are in your network-marketing organization or how long you've been there, ninety days of the *right* activity will create the *foundation for momentum.*
>
> **99**

of these you'll need to do. Even if you're already making a few hundred thousand a year, there may be times when you want to secure an area of your business or launch something new, and you'll need to make a ninety-day run to step up that momentum.

Looking at the five areas of goal-setting I mentioned above, this is what an aggressive ninety-day strategy would look like:

1.   Personal recruiting goals: Ten

2.   Personal/team presentation goals: Fifty (seventeen or more per month). That's fifty quality presentations, four to five

per week, or one per day. Using the 80/20 rule, fifty presentations results in ten new personally sponsored people. (See "Sponsoring versus Recruiting" below, which explains the 80/20 rule.) In order to get fifty quality presentations set, you'll need a list of at least 100 to 200 people with full contact information. You'll also need a solid tool chest and the right verbiage to book appointments, and you'll need to do it with urgency.

3. Personal income goal: This number should be picked based on your compensation plan; however, it's not shocking with a first ninety-day run of sponsoring ten or more (again, see "Sponsoring versus Recruiting" below) that you earn $5,000 or more and lay the foundation for growth and momentum. I recommend that you counsel with members in your business to help them set this properly. If their income goal is higher, like mine was, they'll need to do more presentations and personally sponsor more people to set that level of momentum in motion. (I have personally helped people who had a goal of $20,000 in their first month. They had influence and a big list. In order to reach that goal, they needed to do 100 presentations their first month. They did it; they sponsored more than twenty front-line people and grew their team to the point that it paid them over $20,000 in their first month.

4. Number of participants at event goals: In your first ninety days, the bulk of your number goals should be based on local meetings. With an aggressive plan, set a goal to achieve ten, then twenty, then thirty, then forty, and then fifty. This can be accomplished in a ninety-day period with the right focus. To achieve this goal, your strategy should involve how many personals and how many team members, plus guests. You arrive at fifty by determining who your top

five key people are who could each pull ten or more. This goal also requires a promotional strategy. How will you promote? Phone calls? Social media? Text? Email? Live events? I recommend all of those; however, physical phone calls and excited promotion at live events will bring your biggest return. If you don't reach your number-of-participants-at-event goal in your first ninety days, in most cases it's because you didn't reach your personal presentation goal or sponsoring goal.

5. First ninety-day rank goal: What is the rank that is in sync with your income and recruiting goal? This should be a bi-product of an aggressive presentation schedule within your first ninety days, and you can expect to be the one doing the majority of the work to achieve it. Just make sure the rest of your plan supports this goal, and that you are communicating with a key person in your up-line to help you accomplish it.

Phase Two: Mid Term Goals—Four to Twelve Months (Creating Momentum)

During this period, you'll identify the people you're going to run with while you're continuing with your personal recruiting and width goals. Out of your ninety-day period, there will be a number of people who will come on your team, and you'll have to learn who to run with. This is critical, so please get this: Generally, a big reason someone doesn't

> **Work with the Right People:** Generally, a big reason someone doesn't hit their goals in network marketing is because they spend their time working with the wrong people.

hit their goals in network marketing is because they spend their time working with the wrong people. As you're trying to hit a goal within a certain period of time, it's very important that you don't lower your standards to run with someone who does not meet the mark for occupying your time, rather than continuing to look for the right people. You must learn how to do two things:

1. Get your team to lead you to the right people.

2. Identify your "ideal running mate." In your first three to twelve months, it's critical that you identify three to five people that you're going to invest time in while you're continuing to complete your personal and recruiting goals. Remember in chapter one we talked about Tony's model of ADOME that he uses to determine who he invests his time and energy with, and on pages 29-30 we described the PERFECT network marketing candidate for you to spend your time with.

When it comes to personal recruiting goals, every solid six-figure income earner I have worked with has personally sponsored forty or more people. Now, notice I said they "sponsored" forty or more people. They didn't just recruit them or "sell them" on an idea. Let me illustrate that with another of my "versus" concepts:

Sponsoring versus Recruiting

People say to me quite often something like: "I've sponsored twenty people in the business, and I don't have any results." My first question to them is, "Did you recruit them into the business, or did you actually sponsor them?" People can often sell products or sell an idea to their friends and convince them to take a chance. The reality is, until you learn how to sponsor someone, you have nothing. Sponsoring takes place when you bring the person through a process where they actually tie this business to a *life goal* they want to accomplish, and that's why they're doing it. In other words, they become clear as to what's in it for them, and they make an emotional decision that participating in what you are offering is in their best interest. The clearer they get (the more belief they have), the more excited they get and the more action they take.

Shifting from recruiting to sponsoring is often one of the biggest breakthroughs for people in this business. In the example I just used, most recruit eighteen of their friends, and they may actually sponsor two. Therefore, their judgment of what is or is not working should only be based on the number two, not twenty.

Let me help you get an even better perspective on the number of people you sponsor. In my book *Now You Know,* I talk about the law of the 80/20 rule:[6] If you fail 80 percent of the time long enough—you win! If you understand this law, it will be the foundation for any momentum you will ever create in a sales career. In network marketing, it's a law that, when applied, will propel your business to great heights or that will severely stifle your growth and income when you don't understand and apply it.

When you apply the 80/20 rule to the forty people you personally sponsor, you're going to end up identifying eight different teams that you could build. Out of those eight, though, you're extremely likely to end up with two or three great teams. The average six-figure income earner in our industry only has two to three teams they're working with that are really growing.

People often mentally quit in this industry when they sponsor forty and then thirty-seven of those teams end up not doing anything. The magnitude of that is loaded with discouragement and mental frustration. However, I process that in an entirely different way. Here's the way I look at it: *I need to go sponsor forty people, and I have to quickly identify the thirty-seven I'm not going to work with.* As a leader, my brain works differently than the average person who doesn't succeed in this business. I expect people to quit. As a matter of fact, I believe that thirty-seven of them are *supposed* to quit. That may sound negative; and yet if I accept that as a truth, I never get

---

6   The 80/20 Rule states that 80 persent or your productivity comes from about 20 percent of your efforts.

mentally disturbed when it happens. It allows me to stay focused on finding the three who won't quit. The truth is, I actually end up with a better percentage than that now. I don't think anyone ends up with more than 25 percent of any number they recruit. For some reason, though, that's just a hard concept to grasp for most people.

As you're setting your goals, then, especially during the mid-term piece (four to twelve months), remember to apply the 80/20 rule and allow that in your numbers.

So let's put this into play:

1.   Personal recruiting goals. Yes, I believe that if you want to be a strategic networker and an effective leader, you will need to sponsor (not sell) at least forty people. So if you were sitting down with me after month three and you had sponsored ten already, I would tell you that your personal recruiting goal should be to sponsor thirty more in months three through twelve. And this would be a part of our regular goal-setting conversation until you achieved this.

2.   Personal presentation goals. Since you'll also be helping your new members, you'll find that fifteen or more presentations per month for yourself is a solid number to continue with; in fact, it's necessary to ensure you achieve your recruiting goals. This is often where you will need to develop some people skills to make sure you're taking advantage of all the opportunities that come to you from day to day when you meet quality people. As a strategic network marketer, you must also realize just how many people you have connections with and how those connections can lead you to others.

In my first year of building my network-marketing business, I was driving by a car dealership where just a few years earlier I had met a guy while I was working for a finance company. At the time, I was in my early twenties and was calling on the dealership. This person had talked to me about a network-marketing business he was in; however, in the end I left the dealership and never heard from him again. Fast forward four years later. I was driving by, and I didn't even have a name or a number; I just had a memory of this person. I was now in the middle of a ninety-day run in my first year, so I pulled in and walked up to the front desk. I said to the lady, "Ma'am, I was in here about four years ago and met a salesman who had red hair and was a nice guy. Do you know if he is still here?" She said, "You must be talking about Roger." She continued, "Roger now owns a mortgage company in town named Friendly Mortgage." So I looked up the phone number and cold-called Roger. When he answered the phone, I said "Hey, Roger, you may not remember me, but we met a few years ago and talked business. I was impressed with you and was running through town and thought of you. I'm not sure if you'll be interested, but I have a new project I'm working on and would like the chance to get with you for a few minutes to give you some information. May I swing by?" Roger said yes, so I went by; he ended up signing up, and over the next few years Roger and I built a team of over 10,000 people. The bottom line is, you already know or will meet enough people to build your business. You just have to be clear.

3.   Your personal income goal. This one-year goal should be in harmony with your values. In most cases, those of you reading this book are looking for a six-figure income. Now, I will say that arriving at six figures and maintaining that amount sometimes require different strategies. We'll cover the maintenance strategies in phase three.

Let me ask you a question: If you want to make $100,000 a year, how much do you think you need to make the first month? The reality is, you would only need to make about $1,500 or $2,000 your first month to be on track to make $100,000 your first year. A lot of people don't understand that, because they don't understand the power of momentum and growth.

Here's what I mean: I think it's fair to say that when you have momentum, you will hit your goals. So let's build your plan, mentally at first, to support momentum. If you earned $10,000 in your first ninety days, $20,000 in your second, $30,000 in your third, and $40,000 in your fourth, you would arrive at $100,000 at the end of the year. It only makes sense that if you are truly strategic and you are building momentum, each quarter should grow.

What I want you to understand, however (and the sooner, the better), is that there is a roller-coaster effect taking place that messes with people's heads. Let me explain: If you made $10,000 in the first quarter, wouldn't it be safe to say that you could have earned $2,000 your first month, $3,000 your second, and $5,000 your third (20 percent, 30 percent, and 50 percent, respectively, of the $10,000)? Then, following our example and those percentages, your fourth month you would make 20 percent of $20,000, or $4000; your fifth month 30 percent, or $6,000; and your sixth month 50 percent, or $10,000. What just took place was the roller coaster. In month four, you made less than in month three. This is where people freeze and panic, rather than sticking with their strategy, and it kills almost all momentum they created. Now this illustration isn't an exact science, and yet it's not far from what you can expect when you go all in. Here's a map of how your first twelve-month $100,000 could look like. Get ready for the *ride!*

Quarter 1 - Goal $10,000			Quarter 2 - Goal $20,000		
Jan	Feb	Mar	Apr	May	Jun
Month Goal $2,000	Month Goal $3,000	Month Goal $5,000	Month Goal $4,000	Month Goal $6,000	Month Goal $10,000

Quarter 3 - Goal $30,000			Quarter 4 - Goal $40,000		
Jul	Aug	Sep	Oct	Nov	Dec
Month Goal $6,000	Month Goal $9,000	Month Goal $15,000	Month Goal $8,000	Month Goal $12,000	Month Goal $20,000

4. Number of participants at events. It has been my experience that when an organization has fifty or more people attending a quality national event and one hundred or more attending a regional or local event, they have a solid team in the making and are on the verge of or already are earning a six-figure income. At this point, your numbers are large enough that you are no longer trying to motivate everyone. There are other elements in play, as well. When I'm counseling someone who is in this phase of their business (phase two), we are always shooting for fifty to one hundred at events. It's a game changer. We'll talk more about this in chapter five, when we talk about events as a force multiplier.

5. Your rank goal. This is really simple. What is the key rank in your company that represents a six-figure income? This rank should be represented on your results board; and your presentation, sponsoring, and numbers-at-events goals should all be in alignment with this goal. Understand that

it sometimes takes a longer or shorter amount of time, but a hard twelve-month run will usually set in motion a rank that results in a six-figure income. However, you must make sure that you are course-correcting along the way.

Phase Three: Long Term Goals—Twelve to Twenty-Four Months (Solidifying your Organization)

Phase three is where real leadership kicks in. The five overall goals and the strategies for those goals will vary from leader to leader at this point. You will certainly keep setting sponsoring, presentation, income, number-of-participants-at-events, and rank goals, and yet you will be much more strategic with your time. Regular counseling and attitude adjustments will be a *must*, because of the amount of people you will be dealing with. Some will need to sponsor many more, and some none. So, really, the rest of this book is dedicated to helping you discover your strategy for solidifying a six-figure or higher income with influence and lifestyle. The other side of achieving this is what most refer to as *freedom*.

We've talked about determining what your number is—that amount of monthly residual income that would enhance every area of your life. Let's say your number is $5,000 to $150,000 a month. So what would it take to get to that number in a twelve- to twenty-four-month plan, and how would you solidify that amount? Let me start by sharing another one of my "versus" concepts:

Networking versus Pin-Working

Just because you hit a pin level does not mean your organization has arrived. Focusing only on hitting pin levels is a short-term goal—not a long-term strategy. Most of the time it takes twelve to twenty-four months to build an organization, and it's going to take another twelve to twenty-four months to solidify it; so you're looking at two to four years to build a solid organization.

Here's one way I illustrate this point: Let's say someone hired you to build an NBA basketball team and they put $50 million in the bank for you to use. You could go buy five really good players for that amount (you hit the pin level), but that does not mean you have a great team. It will likely take a few years for the team to solidify and learn how to work together before they can become a championship team. It takes time. People have to learn to trust each other, and they all have to grow until they get on the same page. The good news is, in your network-marketing business you can make money all along the way as you're solidifying. You just have to treat it like a real business.

Generally speaking, you should be able to develop a six-figure income within twelve to twenty-four months. There's only one caveat: You have to be at the right place in your personal development (effectiveness skills). In order to attract the right caliber of people and communicate with them properly, you have to have confidence, self-esteem, and people skills. For example, if on a scale of one to ten you're a two on your communication skills, you'll have to work on that before you will ever be able to realize the numbers we're talking about. And the same applies to your team. If you have someone on your team whom no one likes, you can't just tell that person, "Go do these activities for twenty-four months, and you'll be at a six-figure income," You have to allow some room for personal growth first. It could happen simultaneously while they're building if they acknowledge that they need to grow and are willing to invest the time to do so. You can't change what you won't acknowledge.

Bottom line is, it takes twelve to twenty-four months *after* you have decided that you're really going to grow in these areas. Growth is a pre-requisite for success in this industry, just as a bachelor's degree is a pre-requisite for starting and succeeding in most careers outside of network marketing. Some people enter our industry who have already worked out all those rough edges. They're well respected, they know how to handle themselves around people, and they already know how to think strategically. So when they come into network marketing, they're ready to take off; they'll be able to take the principles from this book and build a rock-solid business in twelve to twenty-four months. Other people may not have experienced much success in life, or maybe they're young and haven't had the opportunity to grow. They will need to read this book and do what we recommend, and they will also need to understand that they will have to go through some personal development before people will react to them the right way.

> **"Income Follows Growth:** Generally speaking, you should be able to develop a six-figure income within twelve to twenty-four months after you have decided that you're really going to grow in the areas of confidence, self-esteem, and communication and people skills. **"**

Remember the exercise I mentioned in chapter one (page 26), where I stand in front of the room and ask people what the characteristics of an ideal leader are? Go back and look at those characteristics and rank yourself on each one on a scale of one to ten. There are other characteristics, of course; however, that's a good starting point for determining where you are in the area of personal development.

After your organization is solidified, your role shifts and you go into the next phase.

Phase Four: Legacy Goals—Twenty-Four to One Hundred and Twenty Months (Creating Wealth)

When you've reached this level, you have worked your way all the way through to mastery. You're no longer doing one-on-one meetings at Starbucks. Now you're planning conventions and events—ways to touch large numbers of people—and you're spending quality time coaching and developing your key leaders. When the majority of your time is invested into leadership, that's when you really begin to create wealth.

At this point your strategies include constantly reviewing goals, coaching with the right up-line leaders, and course-correcting. As you set new goals to raise up and solidify your leaders, you start teaching them the things we've written in this book. This is not a tactical book, although there are some tactics in here. It's a principle-based strategy book; and it truly needs to be the basis of everything you teach to your leaders, because it's built on safe, sound principles that will stand the test of time.

In this phase of your business, one of your key strategies will be to consistently monitor the width and depth of your team. In most compensation plans, your profitability is based on your width and your security is based on depth (the deeper your organization grows, the more secure it is). If you only had one leg of business, you wouldn't be too profitable, because your largest commissions, of course, come from those

> ❝ **Investing Time in Leadership:** When the majority of your time is invested into leadership, that's when you really begin to create wealth. ❞

you personally sponsor. Generally speaking, though, you want to be wide enough so that when things happen—divorces, deaths, someone decides to go to a different company, etc.—you have enough backup teams that the adverse effects on your organization will be minimal. So you monitor that to see, for example, if you need to spend some time solidifying a particular leg or personally sponsoring someone to go wider.

It's very important for the top executives of any successful business to systematically review the organization's goals regularly, and then have an annual review with each of their top leaders about their goals. A leader of a successful network-marketing organization should do no less. To build a massive organization in network marketing, you have to become goal-oriented. As a leader, you will *constantly* get questions about goals, and you don't want to just give a standard answer. Your people need to customize and own their own goals.

Knowing Your Top Ten Leaders

I've learned that being in tune with the roller-coaster effect within my top ten leaders is a key strategy. I can help them navigate through that to ensure they reach the legacy phase. This is not only a key to profitability; it's also a key to avoiding unnecessary pitfalls that may come. Now, for this to work properly, your top ten must respect you, and that only comes from being in the trenches with them and helping them navigate. If they resist, then there are some leadership issues you'll need to overcome, which we'll cover in chapter six.

Counseling

And finally, one of the keys to successfully developing a strategic approach to goal setting is proper counseling. Reviewing your goals monthly and diving deep into them quarterly with someone you trust is a must. Unfortunately, many view counseling as a sign of weakness; and yet when you think about it, the most powerful people in the world (the president of the United States, for example) surround themselves with constant counsel. So here are a few things to think about:

Who you should counsel with:

Is this person someone you respect?

Has this person accomplished what you want to accomplish?

Are this person's values in harmony with yours?

Is this person in the trenches working, or are they retired?

Do you feel better when you speak with this person?

Who you should counsel for: Remember in chapter one we talked about who you should invest your time with (the PERFECT candidate, pages 29-30). We suggest you go back and review that information.

Is this person working the business or looking for motivation, or do they just want you to do their work for them?

Are this person's values in harmony with yours?

Do you enjoy taking this person's calls, or do you find yourself wanting to avoid them?

Is this person committed to growing through reading, attending events, etc.?

Are you just settling for someone to counsel, or do you need to sponsor new people?

It's very important that you answer these questions honestly, because the right kind of counseling often either sets all of your goals strategies in motion or stops them in their tracks. Counseling is the ultimate strategy.

By following the principles we've given you in this chapter, you can develop the extreme clarity you must have before you can go on to successfully develop the other two legs of the stool that will lead to your success—focus and execution. Clarity will show you what you need to focus on, which will provide the roadmap that will guide your execution.

VIPs

☐ Clarity: If you want to be a higher achiever in the network-marketing business, you must have clarity in three areas—your values, your dreams, and your goals—and ultimately all three must be in alignment.

☐ Values: What you value should be the foundation for your goals, both personally and professionally.

☐ Dream and Belief: One of the differentiating factors among leaders is the unique ability to transfer dream and belief when they're communicating with their people.

☐ Alignment with Corporate Values: In order to succeed at the very top level in this industry, you must align your values with the corporate values of the company you work for.

☐ Dreams: Putting actions to your dreams and influencing others to do the same is like adding rocket fuel to your business engine.

☐ Dreams to Goals to Strategies: Dreams without goals will virtually never see progress, and goals without strategies will seldom see real results.

☐ Balance Wheel of Life: In the balance wheel of life, it's not about having perfect balance. The ultimate goal is having a constant focus, being aware, and being intentional about achieving balance in the six areas of life.

☐ Who You Become: If you want to be stable, exceptional, and ongoing in this business, we believe that who you become should be a huge part of your dreams and goals.

☐ Goals: Your network-marketing goals should add value to all areas of your life.

☐ Strategic Approach: How you approach goal-setting in the four phases of your business will determine your daily focus and thus your ability to ultimately execute your goals.

☐ Ninety-Day Run: No matter where you are in your network-marketing organization or how long you've been there, one to three months of the right activity will create the foundation for momentum.

☐ Work with the Right People: Generally, a big reason someone doesn't hit their goals in network marketing is because they spend their time working with the wrong people.

☐ Income Follows Growth: Generally speaking, you should be able to develop a six-figure income within twelve to twenty-four months *after* you have decided that you're really going to grow in the areas of confidence, self-esteem, and communication and people skills.

☐ Investing Time in Leadership: When the majority of your time is invested into leadership, that's when you really begin to create wealth.

Self-Evaluation

On a scale of 1 to 5, with 5 being the highest, rate yourself on the five issues below to determine where you are in having extreme clarity in your life and business.

1. I know what matters most to me, because I have identified the ten values that are most important in my life.

2. I have created and maintain a results board that represents my dreams and goals, and I look at my results board every day to keep me motivated and inspired.

3. I have established at least forty values-based goals; I have put time frames on them and categorized them according to the balance wheel of life; and I have prioritized my top three one-year, three-year, and five-year-or-more goals.

4. I have identified the phase (short-term, mid-term, long-term, or legacy) my business is in currently; and in addition to the forty goals mentioned in Number 3 above, I have set weekly, monthly, quarterly, annual, three-year, and five-year goals in the five specific network-marketing-related goals (sponsoring, presentations, income, number of participants at events, and rank) for the phase I am in.

5. I am doing something every day to grow in the areas of confidence, self-esteem, and communication and people skills.

## Chapter Three

Focus

The question is not whether you can hit your goals; more importantly, it's whether you can stay focused long enough to achieve them. Lack of focus is the single biggest contributor to failure in network marketing, and to success in general.

In the third layer of becoming a strategic networker, we will dissect focus and see how it impacts your ability to get results that will take you to the very top level of your network-marketing business. Focus will help you identify and concentrate on what really matters for the success of your vision and will help you filter out distractions that hinder its progress.

When I (Ryan) was first starting to see some success in my network-marketing business, I realized that the plates I was spinning in my business were messing with my ability to focus. I would go through most days feeling like I wasn't accomplishing what I really needed to get done, and that I had reached a lid on my potential that I just couldn't break through. That's when someone handed me the book *The Power of Focus* by Jack Canfield. At that point, it helped create a breakthrough for me mentally. I realized for the first time that I was letting the things around me dictate what I was focused on, and that I was not in total control. I truly believe now that unless someone can learn to master their focus, they will likely *never* achieve greatness.

I also learned that most people need more than one break-through in the area of focus. My second breakthrough came when I was able to spend my first day in Tony Jeary's *Success Acceleration Studio*. We accomplished more in that day than I could have achieved in weeks by myself, and it was an extreme example of what the power of focus can bring. That's why this book is so powerful. It effectively brings Tony's proven methods to the net-work-marketing world, and I can honestly say that the principles in this book will help you develop the network-marketing business you want in record time.

Understand that you and your team most likely have a *focus* problem, which will disrupt even the simplest tasks, promotions, and goals. Lack of focus will cause people on your team to blame the compensation plan, the products, and the training, when it is actually just a matter of life getting in the way.

Here are a few problematic focus identifiers that I've come across over the years. In essence, you or your team might have a focus problem if:

1. You have a big list of contacts, and yet you can't seem to find any time to make calls.

2. You come home from a great convention with big plans; however, you never seem to take action.

3. You work hard for two weeks and then pause for a week, disrupting all momentum.

4. You have attended every training, read the books, and lis-tened to the audios, and yet you still aren't working.

5. You constantly set activity goals that don't get completed.

6. Your income has been stagnate for the past two years, de-spite your efforts.

7. Your family activities, fixing things around the house, and everyday tasks fill your days, and you have no time for your business.

These are just a few; however, you get the idea. Extreme focus solves all of these challenges and much more.

Getting superior results faster (quickly getting to the long-term and legacy phases we discussed in the last chapter) is critical to your success. Focus is a huge piece to the puzzle for getting results in an accelerated timeframe, and we know that's what you want. Focus is the opposite of distraction, and it is crucial for every high achiever. It takes an intentionally focused person to minimize distractions.

This is the single most impactful area that has the greatest opportunity for improvement in your business.

> **Focus:** Focus will help you identify and concentrate on what really matters for the success of your vision and will help you filter out distractions that hinder its progress. This is the single most impactful area that has the greatest opportunity for improvement in your business.

business. Our hectic speed of life makes it easy to get side-tracked. You lose focus and often don't even realize it until you and your organization begin to suffer. Frequently, the difference between someone who is successful in this business and someone who isn't is focus. You really do get more of what you focus on.

Focus is not something that comes naturally for most people. It's a skill that must be learned, polished, and practiced. It is mental discipline—the thinking skill required to really get the results you want. Throughout my career I (Tony) have developed several very powerful and useful tools for improving focus, and I've helped many leaders take their businesses to the next level by teaching them the principles behind these tools.

When it comes to focus, we want to introduce you to three strategies, and we will break down their applications for the strategic networker.

The first strategy, MOLO (More Of, Less Of), can seem like magic, because it can literally change your life. Basically, it's a simple process for helping you or your organization focus by eliminating activities you shouldn't be doing and identifying activities you should be doing. You want to determine what you want *more of* and what you want *less of,* and then you need to determine *what you need to do more of* and *what you need to do less of* in order to get there.

The second strategy we're going to share is one of the biggest foundational pieces of the entire network marketing success puzzle—and that is *High Leverage Activities.* Your success truly hinges on your ability to cut through the clutter, drown out the noise, and focus on the *High Leverage Activities* that are the backbone of reaching your vision for success in your business.

The third strategy we're going to talk about is another aspect of focus that is critical in this industry, and that is finding those people you need for the three types of *inner circles* that will take your business faster down the pathway to mastery.

MOLO

Strategy No. 7 VIP: Determining regularly what you want to do *more of and less of* is a focus secret of the top earners.

Years ago I (Tony) wrote a book called *How to Gain 100 Extra Minutes a Day.* Over time, that book has been condensed into the MOLO concept. MOLO is an extremely impactful audit of your life that allows you make a better investment of your time. You can do this not only for your professional life, but for your personal life, as well; in fact, you need to MOLO your personal life first to make sure what you want more of and less of reflects your values. Then identify the results you're looking for in your network-marketing business to ensure they support what you want more of.

Finding out what you really want more of and what you want less of, as well as what you need to do more of and less of, is an important strategic life move, and you can be sure that it will result in a breakthrough. Here's the exercise: On a sheet of paper, draw a line down the middle, making two columns. Label the first "More Of" and the second "Less Of." Doing it on your phone works just as well and could be even better, because you could look at it often as a reminder.

More Of

In the "More Of" column, list what you need to start doing more of to get the results you want. These are the actions that will move the results needle. It could be something like developing leaders. Maybe you're doing that sometimes, but you need to do more of it.

Or maybe you need to spend more time working on a strategy to achieve your goals, updating your results board, or getting better at advance planning for your events, or perhaps you need to schedule more fun times with your family.

This is also where the focus part of your career can visibly tie together with your goals and strategy. Often it's the MOLO exercise that keeps snapping you back to the goals and strategies you've set forth. After all, isn't that what we want more of? Also, if you do this on a regular basis, it can serve as a course-corrector for your strategies and goals. Sometimes when we approach a goal we initially set, we realize it's not what we thought it was. MOLO can help fix this.

Less of

In the "Less Of" column, list things you need to move out of your life. That may be something like procrastination or negative thinking, or it could be spending time with the wrong people. It may be "selling" instead of sponsoring or investing too much time looking at short-term goals (like pin levels) instead of long-term strategies. This part of the exercise can also be a big stress reliever—just writing it out can help release it from your mind and help you move on. (See the MOLO template on the next page.)

MOLO is actually a productivity issue, and it keeps the emotion in your network-marketing goals. When you're out there working on those big goals you set and then get off track, reviewing your MOLO will get you refocused on what you want more and less of in your life and business, as well as what you need to do more of and what you need to do less of. That's a good dialogue to have with yourself often to keep you on track.

We encourage you right now to list ten things you want more of, and ten things you want less of. Feel the clarity and the mental focus that comes from this exercise.

The MOLO exercise is a tool that will not only help you as leader keep yourself focused; it will also help you coach your team into much higher productivity. Actually, MOLO should be the focus of all major counseling between you and your accountability partner (your upline/mentor). It's a leader's primary form of conversation to keep the dream alive within their downline. If they're not getting the results they want more of, it's their strategy that needs adjusting—not the MOLO.

MOLO must be tied with productivity. When I counsel with a leader who is already making, say, $50,000 a year, what I'm really looking for is where they're wasting their time. What do they need to do less of, and how can we redirect their energy to get focused on what they need to do more of?

MOLO (More Of...Less Of)		
What do we need to do more of?		
# — What	Why	Who
1		
2		
3		
4		
5		
What do we need to do less of?		
# — What	Why	Who
1		
2		
3		
4		
5		
What do we need to start doing?		
# — What	Why	Who
1		
2		
3		
4		
5		
What do we need to stop doing?		
# — What	Why	Who
1		
2		
3		
4		
5		
What do we need to do differently?		
# — What	Why	Who
1		
2		
3		
4		
5		

High Leverage Activities (HLAs)

Strategy No. 8 VIP: No single skill or habit has a more powerful impact on results than the ability to eliminate distractions and focus on your *High Leverage Activities*.

Determining your *High Leverage Activities* (HLAs) in life and business may be the number one strategy for a successful life. In fact, *no single skill or habit has a more powerful impact on results than the ability to eliminate distractions and focus on your High Leverage Activities.*

In 2006, my business was booming and I (Tony) wanted to fully understand why so many successful people sought my coaching services and why they continued to retain me as a long-term strategic partner and guide. I wanted to understand the real nature of the value I was providing to my clients so I could document, study, and replicate it for others.

My president Jim Norman (whom I mentioned in chapter one) conducted lengthy, independent, and personal interviews with thirty of our best, long-term customers. We asked them how I had helped them reach greater success (which we defined as achieving objectives established in advance and on purpose). After synthesizing all of the responses, we discovered that we were consistently providing our clients with the ability to significantly accelerate their results within time frames that they had not believed possible. We learned that, through the proprietary processes I facilitated during our strategic coaching sessions, I helped them develop what has since become my *Strategic Acceleration* formula—Clarity, Focus, and Execution—which forms the basis for several chapters of this book, including this one.

Based on those findings, I wrote *Strategic Acceleration* and launched it in 2009. I sent the book to many of the contacts in my database at the time, including many of the clients who had sought my coaching, training, and strategic collaboration services. Several were the leaders of some of the largest corporations and organizations in the world—including Walmart, Samsung, Ford, Sam's Club, Qualcomm, New York Life, Firestone, and even the United States Senate. Many others were successful entrepreneurs, some of whom appeared on the Fortune 400 list of the world's wealthiest people.

Since then, my *Strategic Acceleration* book has been spread around the world and has been printed in several languages. It has been adopted by small, medium, and large organizations as a business methodology, and the feedback we've received from many companies, including many of my Fortune 400 clients, is that the number one takeaway is *High Leverage Activities.*

I define *High Leverage Activities* (HLAs) as "those actions that are most relevant to your strategic agenda, success, and achievement, and that most directly impact the results you need and want." Your ability to identify and focus on these significant activities is the major factor in improving and accelerating your results.

Leveraging your time is so valuable. Success in the network-marketing industry is a results contest, and achieving superior results is based upon eliminating distractions that plague your daily time.

Some examples of *High Leverage Activities* might be setting quality appointments, launching new members, and conducting training calls for leaders. Be aware, though, that there are *Low Leverage Activities* (LLAs) that steal your time, such as doing activities that others in your organization should be doing and chasing down things you need because you are unorganized. You have to get more organized and get rid of those LLAs.

When I (Ryan) met Tony, I wanted to solidify my seven-figure business. I'll never forget when Tony said to me during one of our coaching sessions, "Ryan, what you need is the same thing that the president of a Fortune 500 company needs if they want to take their company to the next level. You simply need to define your HLAs and execute them like crazy." Today, I'm here to tell you that defining your HLA's is really what brings the word "strategic" into the title *Becoming a Strategic Networker.* You could literally take this concept and build an empire with it.

Knowing this, it's very important to calculate out how you spend your time. In general, what percentage of your time do you spend in *High Leverage Activities* and what percentage of your time do you spend in Low Leverage Activities? Take just a moment to answer that question. Think about how much of your time you spend really doing the things that matter the most, and then think of all of the things you do that waste many of your minutes each day. I bet you can see areas where you definitely need to improve.

Distractions, like unimportant phone calls, social media, and personal favors, are a big part of every network marketer's life. If you don't want distractions, you have to set up boundaries. Generally these boundaries seldom say no to the important things; however, they do sometimes say *"not now."* Remember, if you don't set boundaries, you will be in a constant mode of reaction to the people around you, and you will be less likely to get to your HLA's.

Keys to Eliminating Distractions

Let me give you my four keys to eliminating distractions:

1. Make good daily lists. Write down everything you need to do that day, and then prioritize those items. Then look at your

list several times throughout the day and ask yourself, *What's the best use of my time right now?* Look at your value-based goals, and specifically look at the monthly goals that fuel your quarterly and yearly goals. Now make sure your list supports those goals and the HLA's that I've listed below. Of course, make sure that you're not neglecting important family projects and dates; however, you'll be surprised how much can be accomplished when you keep everything on a list. (Think about how much you get done the day before you leave for vacation). For example, if you have a list properly developed, you can knock out two appointment calls and an important three-way follow-up call while you're on your way to pick up the items you need from Home Depot. Remember, it's about productivity, not just activity.

2. Be organized to the max. This one may be tough for some personality types. However, this is an opportunity for you to take your game to the next level. When you calculate how much time is wasted in having to find things over and over, or not being able to find important items at all, you must realize that this plays a significant role in how you're viewed as a leader. Unless you're organized, people won't want to follow you, and you'll find yourself bumping up against your own lid trying to hit the next rank. One great solution would be to hire a personal assistant to help keep you as organized as possible (we'll talk more on this when we talk about creating a *Life Team* in the next section of this chapter).

3. Schedule your time on your calendar! What does that mean? It means you have to learn to say no to certain things; you have to own your calendar, which is really one of the most strategic things you can master. In my opinion, if you want to reach the mastery level in network marketing, you'll need to cut out every extracurricular activity

you possibly can for at least a period of two years and fill that time with team-building efforts. Now I'm not talking about attending your kids' events once a week; however, if your goal is to replace your full-time income in the next six to twelve months, you may not want to sign up to be the coach for the team if it requires five days of practice each week. Now this is a serious commitment, so you definitely want to make sure your network-marketing time is maximized to ensure your trade-off is a good one. Certainly block the times in your calendar when you can't work on your business. If you're working a job, then block out that forty to fifty hours a week. Block out your church time, family time, and a date night. After that, my guess is that you'll still have plenty of time to build your business. You do, however, have to be strategic. Learn to not fill it with every offer that comes down your path. Keep four to five meetings a week; your local, regional, and national events; and your call times locked in, and work anything extra around that. When I sit down with leaders who say they want this business, the first thing we discuss is their calendar, and we see if there are any improper expectations (i.e., are they thinking about it forty hours a week but only investing two hours [see "Time Invested versus Time Involved" in chapter one]?).

4. Constantly audit yourself. At the end of every day ask, *How did I do? Was I really productive, or did I just do a lot of activities?* You have to be really serious about this if you want to go to the highest level of eliminating distractions and get focused on the things you should be doing. Activities don't count! Productivity does! If you want to have great results, you have to manage that.

Activity versus Productivity

Because the concept of activity versus productivity is so powerful, I (Tony) want to share with you the content of a PowerPoint presentation I recently prepared to use as a tool when I'm teaching my clients:

What matters is results, and results come from productivity, not just activity. In other words, goals become reality when you have clarity and focus. Focus comes from HLAs, which guide you toward an intentional, predetermined use of your time.

Goals give you a clear plan and direction. You're busy, whether you set goals or not; however, if you don't set goals and stay focused, you'll fill your time with things other than your priorities. People get up every single day and head confidently in one direction or another. Once they're out on the busy streets and highways, everyone looks so sure of where they are going. It appears that they walk or drive with such intention and are certain of their next step. However, if you stopped any of them to ask where they were going or what their end goal was for their day, many would

Activity versus Productivity: Activities don't count! Productivity does! We're all getting the exact results we should be getting, based on what we're doing.

likely not be able to give you a good answer. That's the difference between the busy and the productive. Do you want to be active or productive?

Let's break that down a little more:

Active, Busy People	Productive People
Appear to be going somewhere	Are actually going somewhere
Tend to waste time with small, minute details, because they don't know what the big picture is. They zero in on one little aspect of the journey because they clearly don't know where the destination lies or if they'll ever get there (they don't know the vision, the goals, or the objectives).	Know exactly where they are going, what they're going to do to get there, and what they'll do upon arrival. They have clear goals and focus on what matters most—*High Leverage Activities*
Focus on action only; don't take time to plan a course of action	Take time to plan a course of action, and then take the necessary steps to implement that plan in order to have the best results
Too busy doing some of everything to plan	Act on focused, specific plans in the right time and order so they can yield more positive outcomes
Talk about all the things they're doing	Let their work do the talking; rely on their past track record (their brand) as a good indicator of future performance and achievements
Waste a lot of time	Capitalize on the time they have (168 hours in the week, less 56 hours for sleep and 12 hours for maintenance, which leaves 100 hours for productivity; how we invest our 100 hours determines our results, and hence our success)
Give "squatter" excuses (they know what to do but don't do squat); spend time creating excuses instead of investing time on positive action in the direction of their goals	Don't waste time with excuses; take focused action; get Xs in their boxes so their goals will become a reality; set their goals, tied to their vision and mission, and use the time they have at any given moment to do what they need to do; ask themselves often, *What's the best use if my time right now?* Note: It's better to do nothing at times than to take an action that is useless and does not produce any results. Step back and think.
Measure their days by how many hours they spend "at work" (it doesn't matter what they were doing, just that they were there)	Measure their days by how much they accomplish

I challenge you to get clearer, become more focused, and execute for extraordinary results.

Let me (Ryan) add to that from a "versus" training I've been doing for network marketers for fifteen years that really exemplifies this key concept of activity versus productivity.

Just because you're actively spending time in your business does no mean you're being productive. You have to constantly analyze what you are doing, and you have to be totally honest with yourself when it comes to results. One thing I say quite often is, "We're all getting the exact results we should be getting, based on what we're doing." My point is, whatever you're doing is producing results, good or bad. Some people think results are only good; and yet if it's not working for you, that's a result too. It just may not be the result you want, because you're not doing the right things.

Here's an example that I call the Law of the Big Rocks, which I talked about in my book *Now You Know*. Look at how this illustration embraces the concept of HLA's.

Let's say you have a one-gallon bucket in front of you, along with some water, sand, pebbles, and large rocks, and each of those elements represent a different activity required for you to get you to the very top level in your business. In the early stages of this business (especially when you're in the first two phases of goal-setting—short-term and mid-term), the water would represent personal growth, using the tools of audios, books, and events. The sand would represent sending emails, returning phone calls, and staying organized. The pebbles would be training and working with new team members to create more volume, and the big rocks would represent setting qualified appointments through your system.

Most new people in this business start filling up their buckets with water, sand, and pebbles. They're very busy attending events, planning strategies, returning phone calls, and training new team members. In fact, they're so busy that there is *no room* in their buckets for the big rocks—the activity that matters the most—which is showing the presentation to qualified prospects. When they put the water in first, and then add in the pebbles, the water begins to overflow and there's no room for the big rocks.

So what do they need to change to get the right results? First, they need to understand the difference between activity and productivity. See, all the activities in the example we used are important, and yet without qualified appointments (the type of appointments where the intent of why you are meeting is in harmony with the outcome you are looking for), those activities are senseless and futile. The solution is actually quite simple: They need to fill their buckets with the more productive income-producing HLA's (the large rocks) first. When they reverse the process and put the rocks in first, they can add the pebbles and sand to fill in some of the voids. Then the water fills in the rest of the voids and fills the bucket without overflowing it. In other words, if they fill their calendar with qualified appointments, they will find it easy to educate themselves for personal growth and make calls to their prospects and team members throughout the day (maybe even listen to audios or make phone calls on the way to those qualified appointments). The results will be an increase in their business, because they are placing an emphasis on the activities that matter the most.

In the later goal-setting phases of this business (long-term and legacy), where many of you probably are, the elements represent different activities. The water might be sending a weekly team email. The sand would represent doing basic training (you should have other leaders doing this, except for your new personals). The pebbles are properly-structured events, and the large rocks are high-influencer sponsoring and leadership.

Defining Your HLAs

The third—and foundational—piece of this section is defining your HLAs, and it starts by knowing where you are and where you want to go. When you determine those two pieces of information, you'll see that there's a gap between them—and that gap should be filled with the HLAs you need to focus on in order to get you where you want to go.

This is a huge piece for leaders in network marketing, because the bulk of what we do is keeping ourselves and our organizations focused on HLAs. I (Ryan) have listed five of the most important HLAs that I see for developing leaders in our industry who want to go to the very top level. You can build a business without all of them—just not a big, sustainable one. In fact, I would say that 80 percent of your sustainable results will come from these five HLAs. There could be more; in fact, I expect you to expand this list and add one or two more HLAs that you can identify for your own business. In addition, once you've arrived at a level where your organization is thriving with *High Performance Leaders* throughout, you're personal HLA's may change; however, these five will be the primary HLA's of 99 percent of your organization.

Top Five HLAs: Eighty percent of sustainable results in network marketing will come from these five HLAs: sponsoring, launching, driving depth, training, and promoting.

Here are the top five HLA's I see for network-marketing leaders:

1. **Sponsoring (dream building):** The number one thing you can do in sponsoring is teach people how to connect their dreams to what you're doing. That's the difference between sponsoring versus selling, as we talked about in the last chapter.

    Most people simply stop sponsoring too soon. Building a blitz (ninety-day run) sponsoring mentality within your group, and leading by example, sets everything else in motion.

    There should be a focused plan on sponsoring for each phase of building your organization: launching, growing, and maintaining. That means you'll need to drive sponsoring several times each year. New blood is the lifeblood of this business, and balanced sponsoring efforts keep the excitement alive within an organization. Of course, sponsoring is a product of proper list-building and incentivized contacting. Sponsoring must be praised and recognized properly for an organization and a team to stay focused on it. When sponsoring is low, it's simply because there is a dream/vision/focus problem.

Sponsoring should be a monthly goal until someone achieves a solid six figures, and then it becomes more strategic. Sponsoring influential people can be taught by teaching people skills, personality profiles, and character values. As your organization grows, you will need to have regular strategic conversations about sponsoring at all levels with your team and leaders.

2. **Launching (starting new members):** Outside of sponsoring, launching people correctly is the number one HLA that fuels everything in your organization. Many organizations are only focused on sponsoring as if that were the total answer. However, starting new members properly is the magic element that creates momentum; it must become a very *intentional object* of your focus.

It's imperative that you have a detailed plan that you and everyone on your team is focused on. That plan should include the entire process of launching—from helping the new members make their first calls to helping them get to a big event. Once they get to a big event, which may take up to three months, they're officially launched.

Now, that doesn't mean you should put the rest of your business on hold just to go launch someone. You have to get creative and look for what Tony calls *Elegant Solutions* so you can achieve more than one objective with the same activity (we'll talk more about *Elegant Solutions* in chapter five, on Force Multipliers). Finding *Elegant Solutions* is how you maximize your HLAs. So while you're going to a meeting in one city, you could have a new person ride with you; then you could be helping them launch their business on the way to that meeting by training them how to make phone calls. Or while you're doing a meeting for one new person, you could invite three other new people to join in; now you're helping three people launch in the same night, rather than just one. Another Elegant Solution would be to use my book *Now You Know* to teach a new person how to launch their business using the seven secrets that determine why some succeed in this business and others fail, under the same system.

In my experience, great launch plans include a balance of the following:

A. What to do. A believable, specific goal outlined for the new member that requires proper behaviors in order to reach it. (Most new people joining your business should review this plan and say to themselves, "This will take some work, but I could do that".)

B. How to do it. A belief tied to the teaching that when they help enough people launch properly, their business will be in full motion

C. What's in it for them. A reward for accomplishing that goal that is recognized properly and financially worthwhile.

D. A tiered timeframe to accomplish this launching focus. For example, "When you do this, this, and this in your first month, you get this, this, and this."

3. **Driving Depth:** Driving depth may be the single most strategic HLA that a leader in the network-marketing business can do. It involves all aspects of building your business, but with a specific strategy of going deep within your organization. We will dive into how to do this more thoroughly in the next chapter; however, know that building a list, contacting, presenting, sponsoring, launching, promoting, and speed all play a role. The simple idea is to work with your team to lead you to someone to work with, and then work with them to lead you to someone else. Then continue doing this ten or so levels deep while you teach by example what to do in all aspects of your business, and simultaneously build solid relationships. Your team will feel you driving the business through them, and this activity alone can cause people to turn off the TV and go to work because of the energy you are creating underneath them.

4. **Promoting (numbers at events):** Knowing how to promote properly and making sure it's baked into what you're doing on a daily basis is an HLA of all strategic network marketers. You should have number goals for all of your events and a plan to work backwards in order to build those numbers, and then promote to achieve them. In the midst of all the sponsoring and launching, promoting often gets lost. One challenge is, there are only so many things a leader can actively promote at any one time. Usually there is some sort of *reward or trip promotion* going on, and there may be a product promotion, as well; however, the main promotion you need to perfect is your event promotion.

   Tracking your numbers for event participation is crucial, because your income is a direct reflection of the numbers you have showing up at national, regional, and local events. Generally speaking, here is what you can count on in a participation/income ratio:

Local Events	Regional Events	National Events	Monthly Income Results
20	15	10	$1,000-2,000
50	40	30	$2,000-7,000
120	100	80	$10,000 ++

Of course, there is no way to predict exact numbers, but this gives you an idea on how to think about them. In addition, as online meetings grow in popularity, you will be able to gauge similar incomes to numbers attending.

The bottom line is, you'll never stop promoting. You have to become a great promoter, and you have to get very strategic about it. You should know how many people are coming to an event before they get there. If someone asks you, "How many people did you have at the last convention?" you should know. If you don't, you're not being strategic enough about what you're doing. Knowing your tracking numbers at all times is an HLA.

5. **Training (personal [life], leadership, and business development):** There is a saying in network marketing: "Put them in, keep them in, and move them along." Most training outside of the initial how-to-launch training is geared toward moving your team along.

Even though this could go on auto-pilot to some degree, it has to be a *High Leverage Activity* if you ever want to duplicate and grow leaders to create a sustainable income. There are three levels of focus here: new leadership training, mid-level, and high-level.

Feeding your group systematically is what helps create the residual aspect of what we do, and therefore it must be a focus. Many people think an organization's system is just about sponsoring; however, there's also a system for development and growth that includes listening to audios on a regular basis, dialing into team calls, and going to events. When everyone on your team is truly plugged into that and engaging in those activities weekly, you're building an army that is systematically growing together and using the tools within the system to help them recruit. When you have a thousand people in your organization, you don't have to run around and train them all. You just plug them all into the system.

Training should not take away from activity, and we should be careful to create the belief in our groups that they can grow *while* they go. The training and teaching happen while they're building. People rarely go to a training and then all of a sudden they get trained enough and start building. Most often, the training affects the people who are already doing the work more than the people who aren't. Balancing this focus is best done by properly mixing recognition in the events so that there is a striving for achievement during the promotion period leading up to the events.

·One of your primary jobs as a leader is to ensure that the right message is circulating within your team at the right time. You don't want to simply throw together your calls and trainings at the last minute. You need to strategically lay out a flow of content that you want your team to absorb. As you circulate within your team, take note of holes in the bucket, so to speak, that the group needs clarification on. This is one of the big reasons you should keep circulating within your team—to hear what the new field members are dealing with.

One of the last HLA's I want to speak about is not one of the five; however, it takes place *during* all of the top five and it should be thought of as a dynamic that creates great effectiveness for all HLA's: Relationship development (quality time for true friendship):

Relationship development is the most overlooked HLA in our industry. There is a real need to just hang with your team occasionally, to get to know them and build bonds with them. This has to be authentic, and yet it is definitely an HLA of the masters. It's your relationships that solidify your future and your security.

I would say that sponsoring, launching, and driving depth are the big HLAs that probably need to occupy 60 percent of your time. Training will probably occupy about 20 percent, and promoting about 20 percent. Relational development, however, occupies 100 percent and is layered over everything we do. It is always happening and never ends. More often than not, when I'm counseling with top leaders in the industry and we're analyzing their business, we find that they've been out of focus with two or more of their HLA's. The bottom line is, if you only focus on two or three HLA's, something is going to suffer. Take, for example, Sally's business. She's making money and her calendar is full with two very important HLA's—sponsoring and launching new members. And although she sees the occasional spark of excitement in her business, it feels like she really has no duplication. What we uncovered was that because she was so focused on sponsoring and launching, there was not enough time being invested in driving depth, high-level training, and promoting. She had difficulty letting go, because she knew she was best at presenting. (This is common among those who get to $50,000 per year and seem to cap.) And because of this, she spent very little time planning events that could take her team to the next level and strengthen her team development. Because the right kind of events weren't in place, her promotional efforts weren't effective. And lastly, because she locked onto people and did all their meetings for them, she wasn't really driving depth and therefore never really pushed her eagles out of the nest.

To summarize, you can get results faster by routing out and getting rid of activities that drain you, by making sure you have productivity and not just activity, by becoming more focused and avoiding your distractions, and by documenting and focusing on your HLAs. As a leader taking your business to the next level, focusing on HLA's isn't just a must—it's a have to for you and your team to reach your potential.

Strategic Networker Strategy No. 9

Inner Circles

Strategy No. 9 VIP: Being intentional about your inner circles determines your focus and potential greater than you realize. Choose wisely.

The last part of this chapter is really about how to organize your life so you can consistently stay focused to put the highest amount of your energy toward your HLAs. This is where a fork in the road usually shows up. One direction points to "your potential" and the other points to maintaining the results you're currently getting, with "increased frustration" over time. It's a challenge that is very common among the best strategic networkers, and the sooner you can begin to think the way we've outlined below and develop your life around it, the sooner your breakthrough comes.

We actually advise that you have three teams, or inner circles.

Inner Circle No. 1: Your Mentors

We begin with the inner circle of mentors you will *seek counsel from.* Virtually every successful person in any industry needs mentors for influence, advice, and counsel if they want to propel both their professional career and their personal life forward. In our industry, specifically, they are the top five people you will confide in about the best way to think and act regarding your network-marketing business.

We'll go into this much more in depth in chapter seven when we talk about mentorship as one of the three strategies for achieving mastery. Suffice it to say here that as you think about who you would select for this inner circle, you need to remember that the results you get from any advice will be a direct reflection of the credentials and expertise of the source. If you want outstanding results, you need to get advice from people who produce outstanding results.

> **Inner Circle (Your Mentors):** Select this inner circle very carefully, because they can either knock you out of focus or keep you on track to hit your highest goals.

Select this inner circle very carefully, then, because they can either knock you out of focus or keep you on track to hit your highest goals. I recommend you consider the following before you begin selecting this group:

1.   Are they in alignment with your values?

2.   Have they accomplished what you are looking to achieve?

3.   Are they actively pursuing goals within the organization you are building?

4.   Do people respect them?

5.   Do you feel better when you are around them?

I believe you should be able to answer yes to all of these questions about anyone you are considering as a mentor, in order to qualify them to speak into your life.

Inner Circle No. 2: Your Business Partners

The second inner circle you develop are the top five distributors *you will be mentoring* within your organization, and this top five list is likely to change as your organization grows.

When you first set a goal to have a hundred people at an event, the real strategy is to develop five people who you can help you pull twenty. The reality is, as you grow your organization, when you eventually end up with 5,000 at a meeting and you're making $1,000,000 a year in this business, you will still be able to point to five people you worked through to make this happen. Even though there may be 100,000 people in your organization, the bulk of your communication will end up being with half a dozen or less key people. That doesn't mean you won't have hundreds of leaders who you know, like, and trust; it does mean, however, that you will have mastered the art of who to put in your inner circle.

> **Inner Circle (Your Business Partners):** As you grow your organization, whether it's to 500 or 5,000, you will still be able to point to five people you worked through to make this happen. Those are the five you will focus on and put in your inner circle.

Your inner circle is made up of the people you communicate with regularly—the ones you build a bond with. These are the people who are in the trenches with you, and over time you develop a trust with. You have to consciously and intentionally think about who you're spending time with; and you have to really understand the dynamics of it, because your inner circle is either stretching you to think bigger and motivating you to build more solidly, or they're slowing you down. Basically, you *become* the five people you spend the most time with. In most cases, you're going to run as fast as your inner circle is running. And as you grow your organization larger, you will either need to grow your key people along with you or you change the key people you're spending time with, and that becomes your new inner circle. In reality, what happens as you grow any team is that you keep raising your standards for who will be in your inner circle.

You can't just *form* an inner circle—you have to build one. And if you tie it back to your goals, that's what really takes twelve to twenty-four months or twenty-four to forty-eight months to build. It takes you that long to get the right inner circle.

Here are a few questions that are important to think about as you're selecting who to put in this inner circle:

1. Who do you trust that has alignment with your values?

2. Who is stretching your thinking?

3. Who has influence?

4. Who is really motivated?

5. Who are the ones you can always count on?

Values are a huge consideration. The bottom line is, if you wouldn't feel comfortable dropping your kids off at someone's house and leaving them all day long, why would you want to spend all day with them? Yes, you'll have business relationships who are making money for you; however, if you have people in your inner circle whose values are out of alignment with yours, it will create a real problem.

A big problem in our industry is that people let egos get in the way of helping those in their organization develop their own inner circles. When someone in your downline starts to develop their own inner circle that you're not a part of, that's actually a good thing. A lot of people get nervous about that, because they want to be in control of everything all the time. If that's you, just know that you will stop the growth of your team by doing that.

It's really important to praise and regularly touch your inner circle. Recognize them and let them know often how important they are to you. It's not all about work; communicate with them constantly and spend time with them often to do things that are not related to the business.

Inner Circle —No. 3: Your *Life Team*

I (Ryan) initially learned of this concept while reading the book *The Power of Focus* that I mentioned earlier. I then came to understand it on a greater level when Tony taught me how to think about my *Life Team*. I have since become aware that strategic network marketers who set up a proper *Life Team* enjoy a different level of results than everyone else experiences. As a matter of fact, the reason we're putting this concept in the book is because we don't know of any highly successful CEOs or networker marketers who have sustained success and lifestyle without building a well-operational *Life Team*. Those who don't have one usually get overwhelmed. If you want to be strategic, this is a must.

Think about it this way: When you're out in the trenches working toward making your dream a reality, there are hundreds of life issues that vie for your time and attention. The air-conditioner in your home goes out. It's time to do your taxes. The lawn needs to be mowed, and those weeds definitely need your attention. The housework and laundry are taking on a life of their own. You have to find at attorney to take care of an issue with your will, and you need to shop around for car insurance since your premiums shot up after your teenage son's fender-bender.

The *Life Team* concept that I (Tony) teach has a huge impact on minimizing distractions. It involves strategically building and nourishing an inner circle (a *Life Team*) made up of people with gifts and talents that complement your own, who give you insights and advice and help you execute. In short, they help you do life well. A *Life Team* extends your ability to get things done, make better decisions, and spend more time building your business and securing your future.

Let me give you an example. People often ask me, "Tony, how do you get so much done? How do you write all these books, do all these courses, serve all of these high-profile clients, and still have such a fantastic family life, live so healthy, and enjoy the world?" And here's my answer: I have a super-strong *Life Team*. For example, I've been able to author over forty-five books because some people on my team have been helping me with researching, writing, editing, and proofing for two decades. They know me, they know my content, they know my thinking, they know my processes, and they know my style. It's important to have *Life Team* members you trust and who connect with you.

> **Inner Circle (Your Life Team):** A *Life Team* extends your ability to get things done, make better decisions, and spend more time building your business and securing your future.]

You have to intentionally hand-pick people for your *Life Team*. These will be trusted, talented individuals you place around you, who can either advise you or actually do things for you to help you execute. They're smart people. Sometimes they're in groups, and sometimes they're individuals; and they all have specific areas of expertise that can be leveraged on your behalf. They can range from advisors to your personal assistant to your air-conditioner man. They can include your dentist, your doctor, and even your jeweler. You see, one of the absolute best ways to get things done and really execute is through other people. And having people in your life whom you know and trust, and who know and trust you, can create a winning situation. Among other things, you avoid wasted time looking for someone who truly has that expertise.

Now, before we go any farther I want to help you really own this. You may be thinking, *I don't want to spend the money.* I encourage you not to go there. Let me share with you a powerful book that sparked my thinking to a whole new level about two decades ago. It's called *Your Money or Your Life.* It provides a formula to help you calculate how much of your life you trade for whatever you're spending money on. You take the money you earn on a non-passive basis and divide that by the number of hours you dedicate to your work, so you can be really clear on how much money you actually make for any given hour or minute. Then you can understand how many hours of your life it takes to pay for whatever you're buying or spending money on, and you can make a wise and informed choice about whether that product or activity is worth the cost of the hours of life energy you would need to spend. It's really a powerful tool that helped me understand that I had been doing that for years—building a *Life Team* around me to do the things I was not good at or didn't like to do, or that I didn't need a particular expertise in, because my life energy was better invested doing the things I enjoy and that I excel in.

Sometimes your *Life Team* members will give you insight you wouldn't have gained otherwise. Sometimes they do things for you so you can execute better or faster. Sometimes you have them do something because you don't like doing it or because you don't have the expertise. When you calculate the investment, I think you'll find that having *Life Team* members takes you down a wise path.

The right relationships allow you to call upon your *Life Team* members at any time. I can text my CPA just about any time and can get a question answered if I need to make a big purchase or I need to make a decision that relates to my taxes. In fact, one of my very best friends is also my family attorney and is a *Life Team* member who helps me oversee all portions of my life. I have an air-conditioner guy on my *Life Team*— someone I know I can trust and who knows my home—that I can call to come over and fix my air conditioner when I need him. And sometimes when I call my plumber, instead of coming out and charging me, he says, "Just do this and you can probably fix it." I recommend that you have a person on your team for every segment of your life.

The first segment of your *Life Team* is your home team. Do you have someone who mows your yard, or maybe a landscaper? I have a landscaper who is also a horticulturist, so when I need something done on my trees (I have 120 on my estate), I can call him and he can tell me the distinctions I need. I also have an electrician, a pool guy, and someone who comes out and puts the Christmas lights up, and then she comes out and takes them down after Christmas (and I don't even have to call her). It's so convenient to be able to tap into people who can make things happen for you on your home *Life Team*.

On the professional side, I have several different attorneys for different needs in my life. I have a trust attorney, a deal attorney, and a general attorney, who has been my attorney for thirty years. I have my CPA. And I have my pilots—my small plane pilot, my big plane pilot, and my helicopter pilot. I have my banker, who is also my friend and is one of my *Life Team* members I can call on any time. In fact, I have two good bankers. If you don't have a good banker, you should find one. And I have several writers and a graphic artist—my daughter.

Now let's go on to the personal segment. You probably have a stylist who cuts your hair. And maybe you have a jeweler. I have a personal coach who has been with me for thirty years. I have two drivers; I so appreciate them and they truly support me. Think about all the different people who take care of you. I even have a guy who works in the Apple store that I can call if someone goes wrong with my iPhone. Think of all the stores you shop in on a regular basis. Is there someone who has waited on you and taken care of you for a long time? Or maybe you have someone inside a restaurant whom you can call to get you in when no one else can.

I also have my health *Life Team* members. I have different trainers who help me every week, and I have different doctors who help me really live at peak performance. And I also have spiritual mentors I consider part of my *Life Team*.

As you assemble your *Life Team,* make sure you have a very organized list of the members on your phone and on your computer. Evaluate your *Life Team* members regularly, and shift or update your players as needed. For example when your kids grow up, you no longer need a child-care team member. Maybe you find that you need multiple attorneys or an additional banker.

Here are my four tips for building and maintaining a *Life Team:*

1. Really grasp the concept of a *Life Team* and see who else could be added to your team to help you reach your goals.

2. Note each on your phone, indicating their role along with their name and info.

3. Build the list through referrals, and upgrade as needed.

4. Make sure you respect, support, and really appreciate each *Life Team* member on your list.

5. Be a person who can really move mountains because you have built, assembled, appreciated, and nourished a powerful team of people around you.

I (Ryan) recall my first hard decision to go down the *Life Team* path of thinking. I was in my twenties, riding on my recently repaired lawn mower one Saturday morning. While I was riding, I kept doing the math in my head as to how much it would cost me to pay someone else to do something I hated (mowing lawns). I ended up calculating that $50 a week would get it done. By the time I prepared, mowed, and cleaned up, it was taking me at least two hours to mow my yard. (At that time in my life, my yard was much smaller than it is now.) Then I began to get more frustrated thinking about the fact that I could probably be doing something I loved to do, or building a new business, or sponsoring more people, thus earning more than $50 extra a week by paying someone else to mow my yard. The frustration escalated when I realized that if my two hours a week were invested properly, it could create a compounding result that would eventually pay me $1,000 or more a week for those two hours. That's when I started to see that mowing my lawn myself was costing me $1,050 a week. About that time, my mower stopped running properly. The timing couldn't have been better. I got off my mower, pushed it to the front of my yard, and put a "For Sale" sign on it, and I've never mowed a yard since. That was over fifteen years ago. In addition, I started applying this thinking to many other areas of our lives. My wife applied the same logic to house cleaning, and she's been able to spend thousands of extra hours with our children because of this decision. Understand that all those shifts didn't happen overnight; but once we began to think this way, we positioned ourselves to gradually build a *Life Team* that now frees us up more than the average person.

A *Life Team* is, of sorts, a way to help you free up even more time to invest in your network-marketing business, which in turn will ultimately give you more money to expand your *Life Team*, and off you go! Now you know how some people make so much money and have so much free time.

You'll not become a strategic networker and achieve the level of success you want in this business until you get a handle on your focus and eliminate your distractions. It's that simple. The sooner you integrate the strategies of MOLO and HLAs, and embrace the concept of the inner circles, the sooner you'll be headed toward the success you're looking for.

VIPs

☐ Focus: Focus is the single most impactful area that has the greatest opportunity for improvement in your business.

☐ MOLO: Determining regularly what you want to do *more of and less* of is a focus secret of the top earners.

☐ HLAs: No single skill or habit has a more powerful impact on results than the ability to eliminate distractions and focus on your *High Leverage Activities.*

☐ Activity versus Productivity: Activities don't count! Productivity does! We're all getting the exact results we should be getting, based on what we're doing.

☐ Top Five HLAs: Eighty percent of sustainable results in network marketing will come from these five HLAs: sponsoring, launching, promoting, training, and relationship development.

☐ Inner Circles: Being intentional about your inner circles determines your focus and potential greater than you realize. Choose wisely.

☐ Inner Circle (Your Mentors): Select this inner circle very carefully, because they can either knock you out of focus or keep you on track to hit your highest goals.

☐ Inner Circle (Your Business Partners): As you grow your organization, whether it's to 500 or 5,000, you will still be able to point to five people you worked through to make this happen. Those are the five you will focus on and put in your inner circle.

☐ Inner Circle (Your *Life Team*): A *Life Team* extends your ability to get things done, make better decisions, and spend more time building your business and securing your future.

Self-Evaluation

On a scale of 1 to 5, with 5 being the highest, rate yourself on the five issues below to determine where you are in gaining extreme focus in your life and business.

1. I have done a MOLO audit of my life, both personally and professionally, so I know what things I currently need more of and less of, and I know what I need to do more of and less of.

2. I have written the five network marketing HLAs in my phone, plus the sixth overriding HLA, and I look at them every day to make sure I'm keeping my focus on the right things as I go about my day building my business.

3. I have made great strides in putting together a *Life Team* that helps me free up more time to invest in my network-marketing business, and I have my *Life Team* members and their contact information listed on my phone for instant access when I need them.

4. After carefully studying the suggested criteria for selecting my inner circle of mentors, I have identified these five people and am in the process of asking them to serve in this capacity.

5. After carefully considering the criteria for selecting the top five distributors I need to mentor within my organization, I have identified these top five and have started hanging out with them and mentoring them on a regular basis.

## Chapter Four

Execution

Execution is really where everything—or nothing—happens, isn't it? What we mean is, if you don't execute, there is zero chance for results! If your team doesn't execute, you, as a leader, have nothing. Our goal for writing this book is to inspire you to take the strategies in the book and execute to the point of achieving your dreams. And it's through this third leg of the stool and the final part of the *Strategic Acceleration* formula that not only your team, but also your income and your legacy, are defined. You can create the greatest plan in the world and establish the most focused goals imaginable; yet if you fail to execute, you're not going to achieve it. It's that simple.

Once you've achieved clarity about where you want to go with your network marketing business and get that pulling power working for you, you've identified your HLAs, and you've fine-tuned your focus, you have to take action. Execution is where the rubber meets the road. Clarity and focus provide the roadmap for execution.

Around the 2007 mark, I (Ryan) was at an all-time high (at that point) in my network marketing career. I was 33 years old and had just received back-to-back 1099s from my company that were over $1,000,000 each. That was also about the time I met Tony Jeary, and I was developing a desire to help people inside and outside of the network marketing arena. I remember Tony telling me one day, "Ryan, you really should write a book. It will take your influence to the next level." When I heard that, my first thoughts were not positive. Although I wanted to expand my influence, and although I knew that being an author was a powerful next step, my mind immediately went back to the English II course that I had failed in college and had to repeat. English and grammar were not my strong points. I remember telling Tony, "I'm not sure what I would even write about." The idea of writing a book occupied my head for quite a while after that. *What should I write? Would anyone like it?* Finally, after more than a year of talking to myself, I decided to execute.

My challenge was that I didn't know how to write a book. What I did know, though, was how to build teams and how to speak. So I decided to take the most popular audio training I had developed, titled *The 7 Laws of the System*, and turn it into a book. It was something I was familiar with. I changed the title of the book to *Now You Know: Why Some Succeed and Others Fail Using the Same System* (a must read for any networker, if I may suggest). It immediately sold thousands of copies and is now regularly purchased as a go-to book by some of the top network-marketing companies in the industry.

This book literally changed my life—not because of the material in it or how many copies it has sold to date, but because it taught me such a valuable lesson: No matter where we are in life, we have to execute if we want to go to the next level. None of the thinking and planning, and none of the success I had had prior to the summer of 2010 translated into expanding my influence through the written word until I actually sat down and started typing. It took me three months to write the book, and now I have a lifetime to enjoy it.

Where are you not executing that's causing you to miss out on a major breakthrough?

What is Execution?

Execution is action at all levels. What does that mean? Good execution is getting things done. Great execution is getting things done fast and on purpose. And mastery execution is about intentionally getting the right things done and getting them done fast.

The powerful thing about it is, the world pays for execution. Let me (Tony) illustrate with a story. In the early nineties I invested years in helping turn around Chrysler. The president of Ford heard about me, and I ended up personally coaching him. We built an exceptional relationship, and we had some amazing experiences. Then in the mid-nineties the top leaders at Ford said "Tony, we'd like to have you help us get the top 200 or so of our executives together in a team-building, synergistic state." I said, "I'm not a team-building expert." They said, "We'll pay you a million dollars," and I said, "I can become one!"

So I jumped in and started studying all of the distinctions about team-building. Then I got to thinking, "Why would they give me a million dollars if I'm not a team-building expert?" So I asked, and this is basically what they told me: "Because you get things done. You execute. We believe you can go out and learn it and make it happen for us." Think about that. Over twenty years ago they paid me a

Mastery Execution: Mastery execution is about intentionally getting the right things done and getting them done fast.

million dollars because I am someone they trusted who executes! The world really does flock to people who execute.

Ryan: Tony's story also reveals a powerful principle for your network-marketing business. When you clearly see enough value for something, you stop asking questions, and you just execute!

When Tony was offered the million dollars, all other thoughts, like *I don't know what to do or how to do it*, stopped. When the reason became big enough, the facts, or lack of belief, didn't matter. As leaders, it's important that we apply this way of thinking to ourselves and our organizations. We have to understand that when people are not executing to their fullest potential, the simple reason is that they don't envision a big enough win to hurdle the obstacle (building their business) they have to overcome. Therefore, they're not willing to get out of their comfort zone to execute. What we must do as leaders is help our teams see the *big win* for them, with clearly defined *how to's* for them to follow, so that execution becomes more attractive.

For example, if someone said, "I don't have enough leads" or "I don't know what to say," and you were able to answer with, "Okay, I'll pay you a million dollars if you can give twenty presentations in the next twenty days," what do you think they would say? "I'm still not sure"? I'll bet not! My guess is that they would say "Okay!" and go to work to make sure it happened. In this example, what changed? They still may not have enough leads or know what to say, but their reason got big enough that their lack of belief didn't count.

Please understand that it's not that issues like learning what to say or developing leads aren't important. As a matter of fact, we believe that when these issues are properly taught and handled, they absolutely can and do help an organization. All of the best companies address these topics. As a strategic networker, however, you also need to dig deeper to help change the mindset of your team to understand their need to make some psychological shifts that will help them. When you do, you'll see much more execution than you're currently seeing.

The bottom line is, we all want results; and results simply do not happen without execution—no matter how much clarity and focus we have. And since we are working toward both mastery and the results it brings, we want to maximize our execution.

The following three strategies sum up and categorize the bulk of how to think about your network marketing execution for yourself and your team:

1. Posture

2. Action

3. Momentum

Posture

Strategy No. 10 VIP: How people feel about what
you say is more important than what you say.

What is that mysterious distinction that's so hard to put your finger
on— the one that causes some people to succeed with a system
while others fail? What is that magic that you as a leader can help
identify and develop within your organization to make a massive
difference?

It's one powerful distinction that's made up of four very important characteristics. The distinction is posture, and the characteristics
are attitude, belief, commitment, and self-image. If you really want
to succeed in this business, you have to develop a presence about
yourself that just naturally transfers dream and belief, and that's
what we call posture. Posture is not only the correct positioning of
your attitude, belief, commitment and self-image; it's also translates
into how you execute your HLA's, and it's the single biggest factor in

> **" Posture Definition:** If you
> really want to succeed in this
> business, you have to develop
> a presence about yourself that
> just naturally transfers dream
> and belief, and that's called
> posture. **"**

determining your success in contacting, sponsoring, and launching new team members.

You could say that without proper posture, the idea of strategic network marketing doesn't even exist. You could also say that the top things distributors say hold them back are all posture-related, and yet they seldom see it that way. I (Ryan) am making the hard case for posture because of the supreme importance of the four characteristics it originates from—attitude, belief, commitment and self-image. And based on my experience in working with many people, where you find these four characteristics positioned properly, you find posture. That's why many of the execution problems people deal with can be summed up with posture.

For example, you'll probably hear from your team that the number one thing that's holding them back is, "I don't have enough contacts." Here's my question to you: Is

> **Four Characteristics of Proper Posture:** When someone has these four characteristics—attitude, belief, commitment and self-image—on the right track, there is nothing that will stop them, because they have the right posture

it that they don't have enough contacts, or is their belief the problem? *Did I pick the right company? Will my friends like the products? Is this really an opportunity I can succeed with?* If it's their belief that's holding them back, then is it a contact problem or a self-image problem (belief in themselves)? In reality, anyone can meet enough people over a twelve-month period to build teams within whatever company they're with. However, if their attitude is off, if their belief is off, or if their commitment or self-image is off, they'll not take advantage of the opportunities placed in front of them. The great news, however, is that when someone has these four characteristics —attitude, belief, commitment and self-image—on the right track, there is nothing that will stop them, because they have the right posture.

As you're in the process of building your team, how you've positioned yourself in these four characteristics *will* come out, good or bad. Great leaders understand the importance of posture—both for themselves and for the leaders in their organization—because it makes a difference. When you have ten people on your team who understand and execute with the right posture, you have a totally different team than someone who doesn't. Maybe they're all good at what they do. They all have an arsenal. They all have a high IQ. They've all read tons of books. And yet those who execute with the right posture have a much higher percentage of really connecting with the prospects in a way that builds their belief enough for them to say, "I want to work with you." And posture compounded over time is one of those massive forks in the road that determines a big organization versus a smaller one.

When you're sharing the idea that you want someone to be part of your team, there's often resistance; and how you deal with that resistance, both offensively and defensively, really is your posture. When I'm presenting to someone, whether they join me or not, they're going to know that I believe in what I'm doing. The right presence (posture) causes people to feel the right way, and they want to be on your team.

Most of you reading this book already have developed a higher level of posture than most, or you wouldn't have sponsored as many leaders as you have. Sometimes, however, when your belief goes down, so does your commitment and attitude; and although you have the skillset needed to present our opportunity, you may no longer be as effective as you once were.

So how do you really begin to develop posture?

You've probably guessed it. You begin by developing your attitude, belief, commitment and self-image. These characteristics are generally developed by the level of your desire, as well as the books you read, the people you associate with, and the events you attend.

You'll probably have to ask yourself (and your key leaders) the tough questions, like:

1. *Is my attitude right?* Chances are, if you or a team member blames your performance problems on something other than yourself, your attitude is wrong.

2. Are my beliefs about the company, the industry, the products, and the opportunity really where they need to be?

3. Is my commitment casual or serious? Am I committed to the point that I believe I could lose a million dollars this year if it doesn't work?

4. Is my self-image strong enough? Do I really believe I can do it? Do I deserve success? Can I lead a large team?

These question are tough, and you will probably be in a constant pursuit of excellence in those four areas throughout your business and your life. That being said, there are some skillsets you and your organization can start working on immediately that are specific to and have the biggest impact on posture in network marketing. When you do, you may all see an immediate return of three, five, or even ten times with

> **Posture Skillsets:** These three skillsets, when mastered, have the biggest immediate impact on posture in network marketing: the first impression, the take-away, and staying in control.

your efforts. I discuss these thoroughly in my book *Now You Know*; however, I wanted to include them here since this is information you need to know as a strategic networker.

1. **The first impression: People do business with people they know, like, and trust.** Most teams will never arrive at any state of true momentum unless they develop a systematic approach to the first impression. What you say in the first thirty seconds is so important. It sets in motion the dominant thought people will have about you and quickly defines how they feel about being in business with you. The first impression you make will ultimately determine the type of people you attract.

   Think about the type of people you want in your business. Then reverse that process and think about what kind of first impression you need to make to attract those kind of people, because that can make or break the entire process. Make sure the first impression you engineer is in alignment with your values and who you are.

   Too many networkers are so busy trying to recruit that they're not having the real conversations it takes to sponsor someone; people only do business with people they know, like, and trust.

   Monitor the first impressions your team is making, and look for these common mistakes:

   A. Too much "selling" up front

   B. Wrong initial verbiage (example: "I just got involved with...")

   C. Creating defenses: Help your team make small, effective tweaks to their verbiage, and watch the number of presentations increase significantly within your team.

2. **Staying in control: Ninety percent of all success in sales begins and ends with staying in control.** The number one way people reveal poor posture is when they

lose control of the conversation after a prospect begins to ask questions or raise objections. Remember, the person who is asking the questions is in charge, so learning the proper way to respond to questions and objections is part of mastery. More often than not, the issue being raised is a simple diversion for what the real belief issue is. For example, if someone says, "I'm not sure I have time," it's generally a diversion for "I really don't see where I can benefit."

In my (Ryan's) book *Now You Know,* I illustrate a presentation method I call the box. This is where you strategically overcome the top five objections you know people might have throughout your presentation. There are only six sides to a box; and when you close five of the six sides, that leaves fewer excuses for your prospect to come up with for not participating. I often teach this when I'm helping people raise their closing ratio.

Sometimes your prospects start asking questions before you even get the presentation booked, and this is where you and your team generally lose control.

When you become competent with these objections, then your confidence goes way up and it becomes easier to remember the main rule of staying in control: The answer to every question is the next step of your system.

For example, when someone asks "How much does it cost" before they've seen the presentation, your answer should be, "There are several ways to participate; however, right now I just want to get you the information. May we get together tomorrow for coffee?

In this example, if someone has not yet seen the presentation, the next step of your system is to book a meeting. If you spend time answering too many questions before the presentation, you'll find that most prospects will avoid the meeting because they feel they have enough information to make a decision.

Realize that you're not evading their questions; you just know that if you answer their questions, they will not get to the full presentation. You're actually doing them a favor by not answering their questions. I often say to prospects, "Listen, I don't want to mess this up; and it may take too long on the phone, so let's get together and I'll go through the details." If they get too aggressive with their questions, then I go to the next phase of posture—the take away.

So here's what I recommend you do, and then strategically teach your team to do, as well: Come up with the top five ways that people lose control of the process, along with strategic answers to teach your team. As a leader, you may already have a style for accomplishing this, and yet you may not be working with your team properly. To get the breakthrough you're looking for, you'll need to help your team deal with staying in control.

In network marketing, we now understand that 90 percent of the questions or objections that come in fall under five categories:

   i. They don't have enough time

   ii. They don't have enough money

   iii. They don't like auto-shipment of products

   iv. They don't like selling (or network marketing)

   v. They don't know anyone who would want to do it (they don't have any contacts)

Because you know these objections might come, you and your team will be more confident if you know in advance how you're going to strategically deal with them. You can even head them off in your presentation so they don't come up. But remember, your goal is not to overwhelm them before the presentation; it's to stay in control of the conversation despite their questions and to book the meeting where you will answer all questions. If you don't do this, you will lose control. When you do it, you will notice superior results.

When you master staying in control, you really send the right belief and self-image signals that cause people to say, "If I'm going to do this, this is the kind of person I want to be in business with." This is posture.

3. **The take-away: People want what they can't have.** Both Tony and I are to the point in our professions where we know exactly what we want, and we believe so much in what we're doing that we're willing to say no to clients if we don't think they will be right for our business. Getting to that point is difficult for people in our industry, because they think they need everyone; their posture drops, and they begin to chase people rather than hold themselves up to a level of professionalism.

    If you're going to execute with any speed and maintain your posture, you'll have to learn to take it away. As soon as a prospect begins to get negative, offer excuses, or ask silly questions, it's okay to take it away so you don't waste your energy. Ironically, this often actually draws them closer. When someone has some interest in what you're doing and yet understands that you don't need them, you become more attractive to them and they begin to listen differently. The more confident you are, the more it translates into a stronger level of posture, and people are no longer limited in their minds as to who they should build their business with. You could say that the "take-away" is the ultimate form of displaying the right attitude, belief, commitment and self-image.

    Tony is a master at posture. He's defined what the ideal client looks like for him, and he says no to those who don't fit that profile. When you're confident enough in what you're doing and why you're doing it, then you deal with people in a self-assured, non-arrogant manner that draws them to want what you have.

A few weeks ago, I watched the way Tony dealt with a company to determine what they were going to pay him. He exercised a tremendous amount of posture when he said things like, "Well, if my fees aren't right for you, then maybe we shouldn't be doing business together. I can just give you some of my books." Then, of course, they came back and said, "No, we want to work directly with you." The way he handled himself drew them to want to do business with him.

The same way that Tony exercises his posture in conventional business is really the exact same way we should think and act in our network-marketing business. In fact, this is very similar to how I handle myself in my business. I remember when posture kicked in for me. I was twenty-six years old, and there was actually a notable shift in how I began to communicate with people. I want to capture that shift for you in this book.

Think about the kind of people you do want to sponsor into your business. (Remember the PERFECT network marketing candidate we described in chapter one: **P**roactive, **E**thical, **R**elational, **F**ocused, **E**ntrepreneurial, **C**ompetent, and **T**rustworthy.) My guess is that you're also looking for these kind of people:

☐ People with the right attitude

☐ People who are either willing to or already have the right belief

☐ People who are willing to commit to the work

☐ People who already have or are willing to get uncomfortable to develop the correct self-image

In reality, these are the things you and your team should learn to do when someone begins to ask too many questions or to tries to put you on the defensive:

a. Evaluate whether they are the PERFECT candidate for your team; if they're not, take it away from them.

   Here's an example of a take-away: "Hey, John, this may or may not be right for you. Why don't I call you in ninety days to let you know how I'm doing?" This sends a signal that you're not chasing them and that you believe enough in what you are doing to move on with or without them. Many times you'll get a response something like, "Well, I'm interested. What is it?" Then you can revert back to booking a solid appointment. The bottom line is, you have now set the tone that you are serious.

b. If they are the PERFECT candidate, you may realize that the timing is wrong and that you'll need to take it away for that reason. In that case, you simply want to end the conversation with their not feeling like they are being chased or that you are begging them to do something. This will serve you well three, six, or twelve months later when the timing is right.

Certainly, having a load of contacts with influence is helpful, and yet it's not necessary for building large teams. This is not hard to develop. In fact, most people, whether successful or not, can develop a list of qualities (whether they themselves have them or not) that are needed to succeed. The hard part is being intentional about who you're sponsoring. Remember, you can sponsor all types; however, make seeking the *right kind* of people your HLA.

Tony is also a master at building and maintaining his list. When he meets people and collects business cards—sometimes dozens in a week—he immediately gives them to his team to enter into his Rolodex and catalog according to industry, strengths, etc. And with each new contact, he and his team ask, "How can we best nourish this person and add value to their life?" In fact, he lives by the mantra his father taught him: Give value and do more than is expected. He often shares things from his arsenal with them—books, articles, great URLs or powerful YouTube videos—and makes it a practice to do *Favors in Advance* (FIAs). Thus, he has a great reservoir of exceptional contacts and high-level clients that he cultivates and nourishes on a regular basis.

This is exactly the practice you must model if you want to be a strategic networker. In truth, you can be strategic in a way that ensures you never run out of great contacts to share your business with.

Finally, posture should never be offensive to people. It's not about being rude or overly direct. It's about transferring your strong belief through your attitude, commitment, and self-image in a way that attracts. The good news is that posture can be learned, and it can be learned relatively fast when the next strategy (action) is embraced.

Strategic Networker Strategy No. 11

Action

Strategy No. 11 VIP: Do it now; the world
rewards people who get it done.

Execution is about taking action.

And when we really take a step back and observe how strategic network marketers work their business, we find that there are three areas that require non-stop action: sponsoring, launching, and driving depth. These are three of the five network marketing HLAs we talked about in chapter three. While the other two—promoting and training—are essential, as well, we wanted to concentrate on the three actions that, when mastered, bring the biggest return on your execution strategies. These three actions will also be the bulk of what you teach and train your organization to do. Think about it this way:

If the majority of your team is fluent in continually sponsoring people, with all the skills that requires (building a list, contacting, having a

> **Strategic Action:** When we really take a step back and observe how strategic network marketers work their business, we find that there are three areas that require non-stop action: sponsoring, launching, and driving depth.

great posture, presenting, following through, etc.), then you have a thriving organization. When this organization becomes fluently systematic in how they launch new members and they put the right amount of focus on a new member, then you have rapid growth. And when your organization matures to the point where the leaders truly understand how to drive depth, then you create exponential growth.

Sponsoring

So how do you strategically sponsor people? It begins with an understanding of the Sponsoring versus Recruiting (selling) concept that we explained in chapter two. Let's review it briefly here:

Most people within your team likely view what we do as selling. Often distributors will say to me, "Ryan I have sponsored twenty people and no one is doing anything." What has usually happened is that they have *sold* twenty people into joining. They *sold* the products or the idea of taking a chance. The reality is, until you learn how to *sponsor* someone, you have nothing. To *sponsor* someone is to take them through a process where they emotionally attach the vehicle or products you are sharing with them with something that will help them accomplish a *life goal*. In other words, they become clear as to what's in it for them, and they make an emotional decision that participating in what you are offering is in their best interest. The clearer they get (belief), the more excited they get and the more action they take. Shifting from recruiting (selling) to sponsoring is often one of the biggest breakthroughs. In this example, most of the time they've actually *sold* (recruited) eighteen of their friends and probably only *sponsored* two of them. Therefore, their judgment of what is working should only be based on the number two—not twenty.

When sponsoring is correctly taught and understood by an organization, then expectations are more in line with the action that's taking place. You don't want your team members upset if they sign up twenty people but only two go to work in the business because the presentation was focused toward selling products. They may have gotten exactly what they asked for.

You and your team simply need to sponsor enough people to achieve the results you're looking for. More often than not, you've simply not sponsored enough people to reach those goals. You think that because you have two or three groups that are growing, it's no longer as important to sponsor. The problem with this thinking is that your people do what they see and not what they hear. When an organization can see their leaders continually sponsoring new members, it sends signals to the field that the belief is still high. Until you have three or more teams that are in massive momentum, with leadership backed by leadership backed by leadership, you still need to set the example by continually sponsoring new people.

Sponsoring 40

In reality, six-figure incomes are usually not achievable in network marketing until someone sponsors forty or more people, and most multiple six- or seven-figure incomes don't seem to show until someone has sponsored a hundred or more. Look at it this way: If you sponsor ten people and three of them decide to go to work, then you have three choices of people to work with. And yet you may not think any of the three are prime choices. When you sponsor forty people, though, you have ten or fifteen choices. And because you usually only need three to five big teams to max out your compensation plan, you can pick the strongest of the ten to fifteen people to run with. That doesn't mean you ignore the others. In reality, this strategy sends signals to the rest of the organization about what they need to be doing in order for you to spend time with them. They see that you have set standards they have to meet to qualify for your time, and it causes those who really want help for the right reasons to step up to the plate. Strategic networker marketers know who they're looking for, and they realize that the more choices they have to choose from, the better their selection as they look for the type of person they can work with. Occasionally someone with twenty years' experience will join a company and sponsor ten and end up with a massive organization; however, you need to understand that it took twenty years for them to know how to sift and sort to end up with their base of ten outstanding relationships that took them to that level.

As a strategic networker, you must understand that in addition to several sponsoring runs of five to ten in a short period of time, sponsoring one to two people every month until you've arrived at the sustainable income level you want is the smartest and most strategic sponsoring strategy you can have and the best example you can set for your people. When you understand this, you also understand that you must constantly run promotions, campaigns, and/or events that will help keep you and your team focused on this HLA.

Another thing about strategic sponsoring is that it involves the elements of learning, experiencing, and listening. The learning part involves an understanding of the four major personality types (we'll go more into those in chapter six) and knowing how to cater your communication style to the person you're speaking with (which is another subject we talk about in chapter six). Remember, the tools you use and the system you teach should all be the same; however, the way you communicate is a personal art form that determines your effectiveness.

The experiencing element comes from the practice you get when you keep presenting. The more you do it, the better you get. The reality is, most people on your team will share your presentation with a handful of people and then spend the next few months analyzing why no one joined, and then ultimately quit. The more strategic thing for them to do would be to analyze what they're doing wrong in their presentation, and then practice until they have improved their sponsoring rate.

And finally, those who sponsor the most people have really mastered the art of listening. Sponsoring is more about the conversation than it is the presenting. For example, if I learn to ask John questions, get to know him and his needs, and find out what he is really wanting different in his life, then when I present the opportunity to him, he knows that I know what he wants. So when I tie my presentation to a solution he is looking for, it clicks. That is strategic sponsoring.

Whatever company you are with very likely has a sponsoring process (a system). In reality, however, most are not using it strategically. By learning and utilizing the concepts we've set forth about sponsoring in a strategic manner, you'll be able to soar and reach the levels you desire.

In the next strategy (momentum), we're going to share with you the "ninety-day run" concept, which accelerates the speed at which you sponsor.

Launching

The next part of you action plan should always involve how you launch people. And although each company is different, there is one thing that is universal: For 95 percent of the new members you sponsor, there is a finite window of opportunity to get them started before they get discouraged and quit. This window is definitely less than three months, is usually less than one month, and in many cases is less than two weeks. So in reality, if you are truly sponsoring people instead of selling them into something, you should have many people ready to get started right away, especially if they've invested into extra product or a kit that will help them. Understand, however, that even though they want to get started, they may or may not be ready to get out of their comfort zone. They're often hesitant (sometimes even scared to death) to pick up the phone and invite someone to sit down with them.

So what's the best way to launch someone?

1. **Show them what to do:** Set short, attainable goals for their first week and first month—something they can

believe in. (Yes, everyone wants their new member to become the top earner in their first month; however, setting
your new member up for failure will backfire. You must be
strategic about this!)

2. **Show them exactly how to do it,** and then help them
    do it.

3. **Show them what's in it for them** and find out what
    they are looking for by joining. (We went into this in more
    detail in chapter three. You may want to review that infor-
    mation now.)

Now, with all of these things in place, understand that everyone
still won't launch; however, a higher percentage will, and that's all
you need. In reality, if just 20 percent of everyone on your team
hits in their first month the lowest rank your company offers, your
business will be massive!

Driving Depth

The last strategic action step is what is known as driving depth (or
tap rooting). It's the strategic networker's biggest secret to building
massive organizations, and yet it's rarely understood. It is systematic, and it is virtually the only 100-percent-guaranteed strategy
that will ensure your success in network marketing (i.e., when you
drive depth long enough, you're guaranteed to succeed).

Driving depth really takes both your sponsoring strategy and
your launching strategy into another whole level. It puts you in
the driver's seat, so you never run out of leads and you always have
a meeting to go do.

First, let's talk about the mindset of driving depth.

1. It counts only on yourself. Whether you're just beginning
    or are in the process of doubling your income, there are
    times when you need to be in charge.

2. It puts your income in your control. You can set your income goal and then use this strategy to show you the predictable change in your income.

3. It sets the right example. You are in the trenches, and people will notice. This is the best way to teach your group—it's much better than calls or meetings.

4. It creates excitement. Whenever someone takes charges and stirs up the energy with action, there is excitement.

5. It is not the same as stacking depth. Sometimes you might place people you personally sponsor under someone on your team. That is stacking depth, not driving depth. Although there is generally nothing wrong with stacking someone, when you're driving depth, you're specifically looking for the benefit of driving from relationship through relationship.

6. It's not convenient. You will work harder than you ever have before, and yet you don't have to neglect what's most important to you.

So what is driving depth?

Driving depth involves using the key action steps of sponsoring and launching to drive a line of business deep. Just think about it as "A to J." Let's say you *sponsor* Andy and you help him develop his list, book some meetings, and show the presentation. At some point, Andy will sponsor a few people and you will begin to launch them. The key here (in driving depth) is that you are the one to launch them; you will not be relying on Andy to do so. In this case, say you help Andy *sponsor* Brandy, and you *launch* Brandy the same way until you help her *sponsor* Charlie. You keep going, all the way through Denise, Eric, Felicia, George, Hanna, Isabel, and John. In each situation, one led you to another; however, you were the one that helped *launch* each person properly. When you're driving depth, you'll help each person set goals, and at the same time you are maximizing each and every meeting as you are teaching all of them how to work the business. For example, when you do a meeting for George, you call everyone else you've launched and have them bring people to the meeting, as well. This creates energy! And when you drive from A to J in a ninety-day period of time, this is usually the catalyst for great momentum.

Another thing that is exciting is that anyone can learn to drive depth. It just requires extreme focus. Here are the skills you'll need, along with your goals, dreams, and excitement. You already know how to do these things; however, it's now time to be more strategic.

Driving depth skills:

1.   Sponsoring new distributors or customers (driving depth works best when you keep sponsoring)

2.   Developing the list (learn to help the new person develop a contact list of likely distributors or customers)

3.   Booking a meeting

4.   Showing the plan

5.   Closing the sale

6.   Handling objections

7.   Teaching the system

8.   Becoming an excellent promoter

You see, you already possess the skills required. Driving depth, however, causes you to be much more intentional about how you duplicate these skills within your organization. When you're driving depth, your team members get to see all of these skills in action and are thus much more likely to learn to do them.

We'll end this section by giving you some specific best practices and things to avoid for driving depth. As you can tell, I (Ryan) believe that driving depth is the action that brings the largest return for your investment. So I recommend that you really grab hold of these ideas.

Here are some best practices for driving depth:

1. When you're driving depth, remember that there is a short *window of opportunity* to begin the process with everyone who joins your team. If you sign up Alice today and you don't help her build a list, contact, and share presentations that lead to sponsoring a few people within the first month, chances are you'll need to start new with someone else.

2. Your first goal in driving depth is to get your new people to make their list. This begins the process, and it psychologically gives you an advantage. When they've made their list, they know that you know they have people to call.

3. Driving ten levels deep in ninety days is like magic. This is one of the most proven methods for creating momentum there is.

4. When driving depth, don't forget about your other teams. Promote events as you're driving, and promote to your other teams so they can plug in, as well. This will maximize your efforts.

Here are a few things to avoid while you're driving depth:

1. As you're going from A to J, you don't want to transfer leadership too soon (i.e., you want to be hands-on until people begin to do meetings without you). In reality, you should not take your eye off the ball for at least ninety days, unless you sponsor someone who has a proven track record—and even then, be careful.

2. Avoid a "this-leg-is-done" attitude. When you're driving depth, you'll often get a spark of business. With your team excited, it would be easy to visualize how this could last forever. What you want to do when this happens is keep driving, and don't let your foot off the pedal. Remember

to run hard for ninety days; then evaluate and counsel on a regular basis, and course correct as you go.

3. You'll want to avoid overly focusing on how many are or are not signing up. Yes, that seems odd; however, if the total focus is doing proper presentations and doing as many as possible, and you're counseling on a regular basis, you'll want to put all your energy into the number of presentations you're doing within ninety days.

And finally, the benefits of driving depth properly are many. Here are the top five ways it builds relationships:

1. It allows you to meet and get to know many people on a personal level. This is gold for anyone wanting to build a really massive business.

2. It creates loyalty. As you develop relationships, you will be contributing to people's success. This creates loyalty for a long–term organization, and it also develops a team environment.

3. Members gravitate to depth-drivers (leadership). As people (new and existing team members) see someone taking charge of their business, you'll notice that they begin to view you as their leader. Driving depth really does identify you as a leader.

4. It gives you influence (leadership is influence). Depth-drivers not only develop influence within their own organization; they also begin to get noticed throughout their entire company. This elevates the way your team views you.

5. It creates an atmosphere for duplication. As you're driving depth, one of the most important things that happens is that you duplicate yourself. Because you are hands–on, you're much more likely to be able to find someone who

catches the idea of what you are doing and begins to emulate (duplicate) it.

What's your Presentation Number?

As you put together your action plan, understand that when you arrive at the level of freedom you're looking for, there will have been a certain number of presentations you've completed to get you there. My experience tells me that this number usually is around 200 presentations; for some people it may take 300, and for some it may just take 100, depending on their level of posture. The bottom line is, you have a number; and this number is all that is separating you from freedom!

However, most people in our industry quit before they've ever done ten or twenty legitimate meetings, so they never even stand a chance of developing themselves through the process. Even if the first fifty meetings you did were all a flop, if you were paying any attention at all, you at least learned fifty things not to do. This is very powerful, when you understand that it's just a certain amount of the right kind of work that needs to be done to allow you to arrive there. If you have a *Strategic Mindset*, and if you have clarity and focus and you execute properly, you're going to arrive there much quicker than those who don't. And those who don't will often get burned out in the process and never arrive.

The bottom line is, everyone has a number; and once you understand this, the only thing left for you do is to pick the speed at which you want to arrive.

Momentum

Strategy No. 12 VIP: The *speed* at which we pursue our goals and dreams affects everything!

Momentum is really the goal. Aren't all the action, all the meetings, and all the strategies done just so we can create sustainable momentum? The exciting part about the industry of network marketing is that in most cases when someone learns how to create sustainable momentum in just two or three of their teams, they can experience a leveraged income that can set them financially free.

I (Tony) believe that inertia plays into momentum. Once something's in motion, it's easier to keep it going. That's why I teach a concept called *Production Before Perfection*—not allowing the fear of perfectionism to stop you from starting. I believe you should start with what you have and then perfect as you go. The important thing is to get the momentum going, because when you go as far as you can see, then you can see farther.

My mentor, the late Zig Ziglar, used to tell a story about a pump. Many are familiar with the story. He literally had a hand pump that he carried on stage when he gave a motivational speech, and he'd pull that pump out and describe the process required to prime the pump in order to get momentum going and get something coming out the other side. You just have to get it in motion and get it done.

So what is momentum and how is it created? Here's how I (Ryan) believe momentum is created and sustained in the network-marketing industry:

☐   Momentum is created when a lot of people win at the same time.

☐   It is created when a large amount of the right activity is done in a short enough period of time.

☐   It is sustained when leaders strategically make the right decisions to bring a new, improved, and improving culture to the organization.

Since I believe those are concepts you should strategically think about and act upon, let's look at them further.

Helping People Win

We help people win when we strategically help them set goals and take action in a way they can achieve them. We reinforce those wins through recognition. We'll go into recognition more in depth in chapter five; however, I want to mention here that I believe there should be two types of recognition within a network-marketing organization:

Creating Momentum: Momentum is created when a large a lot of people win at the same time and when a large amount of the right activity is done in a short enough period of time.

1.   The first type is for the activity. For example, if you run a promotion, you could recognize your team members who have done fifteen presentations in a month. Or you could have a cookout for all of those who share fifteen times in a month. These are just a couple of examples of how you could help a lot of people win in an organization.

2. The second type of recognition is for results. Almost all companies have a ranking system that recognizes results, and there are also team things that can be done. For example, if someone signs up two new customers or members in a week, there could be some special recognition, as well as a bonus.

The bottom line is, when we help a large amount of people win, we win!

Doing the Right Amount of Activity in a Short Enough Period of Time

As you may or may not have experienced, momentum can begin in a relatively short period of time. Keeping the momentum, however, can sometimes be more challenging. Nevertheless, you must have it before you can keep it, so let me give you a couple of proven methods to help create momentum in your organization.

1. **Massive action**

    Most people have never experienced massive action.

    In a previous section of this chapter we laid out the three most important categories of action: sponsoring, launching, and driving depth. So think about what massive action is. You guessed it—massively doing those things that need to be done to sponsor, launch, and drive depth.

    Those who have heard me teach on momentum have heard me say this: "The speed at which we pursue our goals and dreams affects everything!"

    You see, when we do a large amount of work in a short period of time, we don't just get things done quicker; we also get exponential results that lead to momentum. When we sponsor with urgency, when we launch with urgency, and when we drive depth with urgency, we set in motion a standard for our organization that compounds into something everyone thinks is magical—it's momentum, and it can be strategically created.

Let's expand on the idea we talked about earlier, that you need to do roughly 200 presentations in order to be free. The next question would be: How long do you want to take to get them done? And how much momentum do you want to have when you arrive? Here is the reality: Twenty meetings done in twenty months is different from twenty

> **The speed at which we pursue our goals and dreams affects everything.**

meetings done in twenty days. It's the same twenty people through the same presentation; however, the twenty people in twenty days *feel* something entirely different when the presentation is being given than if they were the only presentation that month. They feel the urgency; they feel no pressure, since the presenter is too busy to chase; they feel like something is really happening. This ends up being a really big part of transferring belief to your prospect, and it can't be faked. Somehow, your prospects can tell if your calendar is full or not. They'll know if it's not, because you can't fool yourself and therefore can't help but subliminally communicate to your prospect your lack of business. And they'll know if it is, because they'll feel your excitement and belief.

In my video titled *Move the Marbles,* I teach that you should purchase two jars and 200 marbles and put all 200 marbles in one of the jars. Every time you complete a presentation intended to sponsor someone, take one marble out and put it in the other jar. When you've moved all the marbles, chances are you're free. (Check out my video at ryanchamberlin.com under Free Videos.)

I challenge you to move twenty marbles a month instead of twenty marbles a year. Get through your ground game in ten months instead of ten years. Watch what happens. You'll not only be an expert; you'll more than likely have started a massive movement of momentum.

2. **The Ninety-Day Run Strategy**

There is no better way to kick-start your momentum focus than with a ninety-day run. Anyone can focus for ninety days, and this is a fundamental go–to strategy when leaders on your team really want to go to the next level. That's why for any leader who comes to me wanting to go the next level, my first question is: When was the last time you went on an all–out, massive-action run for ninety days?

☐   This is a ninety-day focus on sponsoring, launching, and driving depth.

☐   This is ninety days of contacting from your personal list to ensure you sponsor your next ten.

☐   This is ninety days of blocking everything else out except church and family.

☐   This is ninety days of promoting every day for conference calls and events.

☐   This is ninety days of communicating every day with your upline partner who is working with you.

☐   This is ninety days of five to ten meetings a week, minimum.

What I've noticed in my twenty years in this industry is that those individuals who are doing five to ten meetings a week for a long enough period of time are the ones who end up walking across the stage. And although you may end up doing more, five to ten is a sustainable model that can be duplicated, even by the part-timer. Although five to ten sounds easy, the challenge is to stay on it for ninety days straight and not miss a week.

If you think about it, within ninety days of doing massive action, you have the beginning of momentum; and within a year of doing it, you can set in motion enough energy that you could spin that plate for the next couple of decades. In reality, I'm still living off of work I did twenty years ago. That initial run set in motion a never-ending chain reaction that led me to where I am today, and yet it took a massive-action run to get there.

When you, as the leader, are doing ninety-day runs, it sets the tone for your organization. Don't lose sight of who you're looking for: When the dust settles, if you end up with five excited people, you're *gold*. You can do anything for ninety days. It's just a matter of priorities—blocking out everything that can be blocked.

My guess is that after you've finished reading this book, it's time to do a ninety-day run!

New, Improved, and Improving

Within ninety days, you really can begin to see the makings of momentum, and yet even momentum needs to be treated right to make it last. The ultimate goal is *sustainable momentum*.

So how do we keep it going? Let's look at how the Fortune 500 companies do it. When you walk the aisle in the grocery story, it's common to see that a brand you're familiar with is launching something new. Every once in a while Apple, Google, and Coke all launch *new* products, because new helps create a fresh, new excitement. Now, understand that they don't do it every month, or it would lose its luster; however, we know from experience that new things create interest and enthusiasm.

Another thing that keeps the excitement going is when they re-launch something as "*i*mproved," like new and improved Crest

Toothpaste. Improved speed on a smartphone sells millions. It's not necessarily *new,* but consumers also love *improved.*

The real sustainable piece, however, is when an organization's followers (whether they are Apple or Coke) recognize and believe that they are in a constant state of *improving.* The culture they have built is always getting better, and people are proud to be associated with it.

> **Sustaining Momentum:** Momentum is sustained when leaders strategically make the right decisions to bring a new, improved, and improving culture to the organization.

So in strategic network marketing terms, to sustain momentum after you've completed your ninety-day run, it's wise to bring something new to the table—like a new goal-setting method or a new promotion. New things (but not too much new) help keep momentum going.

You may also want to improve your methods, your videos, your materials, your communication, and/or your organization (within corporate guidelines, of course).

However, what you really want in your organization is the feeling that everything is going to keep getting better—that continual improvement is a given. If you want to have this culture, you have to be consistent with your improvements. This is how great teams grow for a long period of time.

KPI's (Key Performance Indicators)

When you're strategically and intentionally working to create momentum, and you're in the midst of momentum, there are certain basic things you have to look at, talk about, and adjust on a weekly basis:

1.   The number of presentations you and your organization are doing per week (how many are doing fifteen or more a month?)

2.   The number of *new members* joining your team each week

3.   The number attending your local, regional, and national events

4.   Your profitability (how many checks are flowing through your organization?)

As a strategist, it's important to run your business like a business. And understanding this data will help keep you focused on what is or isn't working. You should not wait more than seven days into your ninety-day run to be talking about these items, and I believe a constant review of them is required. Those four KPIs are really the heartbeat of your business and quickly help you decide the strength of your organization. You are the leader. It is up to you—not your company—to drive the increase of these numbers.

We've talked about how to use the strategies of posture, action, and momentum to achieve the next step to mastery—execution. In chapter five we'll look at three more strategies that will multiply your efforts and help you get there *faster.*

VIPs

☐ Mastery Execution: Mastery execution is about intentionally getting the right things done and getting them done fast.

☐ Posture: How people *feel* about what you say is more important than what you say.

☐ Posture Definition: If you really want to succeed in this business, you have to develop a presence about yourself that just naturally transfers dream and belief, and that's called posture.

☐ Four Characteristics of Proper Posture: When someone has these four characteristics—attitude, belief, commitment and self-image—on the right track, there is nothing that will stop them, because they have the right posture.

☐ Posture Skillsets: These three skillsets, when mastered, have the biggest immediate impact on posture in network marketing: the first impression, the take-away, and staying in control.

☐ Action: Do it now; the world rewards people who get it done.

☐ Strategic Action: When we really take a step back and observe how strategic network marketers work their business, we find that there are three areas that require non-stop action: sponsoring, launching, and driving depth.

☐ Momentum: The *speed* at which we pursue our goals and dreams affects everything!

☐ Creating Momentum: Momentum is created when a lot of people *win* at the same time and when a large amount of the right activity is done in a short enough period of time.

☐ Sustaining Momentum: Momentum is sustained when leaders strategically make the right decisions to bring a *new*, improved, and improving culture to the organization.

Self-Evaluation

On a scale of 1 to 5, with 5 being the highest, rate yourself on the five issues below to determine where you are in executing on the mastery level in your life and business.

1. I have developed and maintain a presence (posture) that naturally transfers dream and belief to my team and my prospects.

2. I consistently ask myself and my team the tough questions that reveal whether we are maintaining the proper attitude, belief, commitment and self-image. I am in a constant pursuit of excellence in those areas.

3. I set the right example for my team by continually sponsoring new members—one or two every month.

4. I regularly drive depth in my organization, going from A to J in a period of sixty to ninety days.

5. I do ninety-day runs on a regular basis to keep up my momentum and to set the tone for my organization.

Chapter Five

Force Multipliers

Network marketing is an industry that is built almost entirely on systems, and your success is largely contingent upon how well you master the systems. For example, there's a system for all five of the top *High Leverage Activities* (HLAs) we mentioned in chapter three: sponsoring, launching, driving depth, promoting, and training. There's even a leadership system. Many people think the secret to succeeding in this business is plugging into a system; however, the truth is, if you're going to break out of that $50,000-to-$100,000-a-year bracket where you're currently trapped, you're going to have to do more than just plug into the system—you're going to have to start driving it.

I (Ryan) believe it's safe to say that virtually all top achievers across all industries are systematic thinkers. In fact, I'm convinced that Tony Jeary is one of the most systematic people in the world. He has created

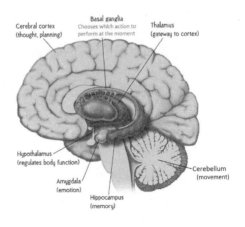

169

a system for executing essentially every concept he teaches to his high-achieving clients in hundreds of different industries—including network marketing. For all practical purposes, the word "systems" is synonymous with the word "habits." So basically, that means that Tony has identified habits (including processes) that support the principles he teaches that will help any leader reach their desired results faster. In fact, his goal for his clients, and even for his own personal and professional life, is to put everything on "automatic." That's our goal for you, as well.

Let me (Tony) share some information with you that really validates my passion for creating systems/habits to accelerate your success: At the center of your brain is a walnut-sized piece of "neural tissue" called the basal ganglia, which basically offloads from the cerebral cortex (the "thinking" part of the brain) any sequences that have turned into systems/habits, therefore freeing the cerebral cortex up to handle other things. So the brain actually craves habits and systems so it doesn't have to work so hard!

According to an article by Brett and Kate McKay entitled "Unlocking the Science of Habits: How to Hack the Habit Loop & Become the Man You Want to Be," scientists discovered this information after surgically placing wires and probes inside the brains of healthy mice to watch their brain activity as they ran through mazes. At first, the mice really had to think about which way to go as they ran through the maze; after many weeks of running through, though, it became more automatic for them. According to their brain probes, they weren't even having to think about it; there was little activity in the cerebral cortex, and even that part related to memory showed decreased activity. In the meantime, their basal ganglia was working overtime.[7]

---

7   Information in this section taken from article by Brett and Kate McKay, "Unlocking the Science of Habits: How to Hack the Habit Loop & Become the Man You Want to be," The Art of Manliness, http://www.artofmanliness.com/2012/11/20/power-of-habits (accessed 6/9/17).

"Since the initial research with mice, researchers have found that habits work pretty much the same way with us humans," the article said. "Whenever we go into 'habit mode,' our brain activity shifts from our higher-thinking cerebral cortex to our more primitive-thinking basal ganglia. It's one of the ways our brain works more efficiently. By freeing up mental RAM from our cerebral cortex, our brains can use that mental energy for more important stuff, like creating a life plan, starting a business, or even researching the science of habits."[8]

Since creating the right habits/systems is one of the top strategies for achieving mastery, we'll go into that topic in detail in chapter seven, when we talk about mastery. However, we wanted to lay the groundwork here in this chapter, because we believe that the idea of driving the network marketing system really is a "force multiplier."

Exactly what is a "force multiplier"? It's a factor that dramatically increases (multiplies) the effectiveness of something you're doing. In the military, it's a term that applies to a capability that significantly increases the combat potential of a military force and thus enhances the probability of a successful mission. For example, if a combat force goes into a particular area at night, night goggles would be a force multiplier that would significantly enhance their chances of a successful mission.

> " **Force Multiplier:** A force multiplier is a factor that dramatically increases (multiplies) the effectiveness—and thus the results—of something you're doing. "

---

8   Brett and Kate McKay, "Unlocking the Science of Habits: How to Hack the Habit Loop & Become the Man You Want to be," The Art of Manliness, http://www.artofmanliness.com/2012/11/20/power-of-habits (accessed 6/9/17).

I (Tony) use pre- and post-workout force multipliers every time I work out. For example, my trainers are very specific about having me eat certain proteins and complex carbohydrates exactly forty-five minutes before I train, because they multiply the efforts toward what I want to accomplish by keeping my energy up as I work out. A force multiplier, then, refers to any factor that dramatically increases your results in whatever you're doing. It's really about creating leverage. Force multipliers in network marketing are aspects of your business that can help create an exponential return. Wouldn't you like to multiply every effort you make toward pursuing success in your business?

The *Elegant Solutions* we've talked about throughout the book are force multipliers, since they definitely multiply your efforts and give you maximum leverage and production by accomplishing two or more objectives with the same action. We suggested several *Elegant Solutions* in chapter three, including:

1. Taking new people with you to a meeting in another town and helping them launch their business on the way by training them how to make phone calls

2. Inviting two or three other new people to join you while you're doing a meeting for someone, thereby helping all of them launch on the same night

Here are a few more:

1. Finding solutions for growth in a busy world, such as:

   a. While you're exercising, listening to an audio on personal growth

   b. Setting an appointment with yourself—and putting it in your calendar—for 15 minutes each day. When it's in your calendar, it's more likely to happen. Let others know you have an appointment, and use this time to read or listen.

    c. Maximizing your driving time. Instead of returning calls while you're driving, make sure you listen for at least fifteen to thirty minutes each day to something that can help you grow.

2. Baking family trips into your network-marketing schedule

    a. You could do things like planning a one-day seminar in Atlanta and staying over an extra day to go to Six Flags with your kids. When they're younger, it may be a little more challenging; however, you'd be surprised at how many babysitters would come along just for a little money and a free day at an amusement park.

    b. Another thing you could do is drive to your vacation destination instead of flying. Then you could schedule a stop or two on your way to support your team— something you otherwise may not have been able to do. You shouldn't do this every time you take a vacation, of course; however, if you have a clear conversation with your family about what you're planning, they will usually be more than willing to give you one day before you shut down for a week.

    c. You may also think about setting family trips as a reward for accomplishing a business goal. If you want your kids to get excited about meetings, just let them know that once you've sponsored ten new people, the family will be going to Disney. Talk about motivation! The kids will be asking you every day how many people you've sponsored! This may be the best form of accountability ever!

The three strategies we present in this chapter—events, tools, and recognition—are the biggest force multipliers of the network marketing system. Let's take a look at each of them.

Events

Strategy No. 13 VIP: People won't usually remember most of what they hear at an event; they will, however, remember 100 percent of how they felt at the event.

Having a proper event mindset is a huge force multiplier in your business, because events are the single best opportunity you have to get people emotionally connected to their business. And the emotional connection is a force multiplier in itself, because the "why" has now been taken from their head to their heart.

This emotional connection is a little different than the "why" we talked about in the chapter on clarity. That "why" is what gives them a clear vision to work toward; we're talking here about the "why" that, when big enough, drives an emotional reason to build their business. It's an emotional connection that solidifies their relationship with the company and with their team, and it can only be accomplished through events. You can't achieve this kind of connection through phone calls or books. When people come to Tony's

The Why: The "why" that comes from events is an emotional connection that solidifies the relationship people have with the company and with their team, and it can only be accomplished through events.

studio, for example, they have a much different experience than when they participate in a Skype call with him or read one of his books. They leave the personal one-on-one encounter with much more excitement and emotion, which fuels their drive for results.

When people hire me (Tony) to do a keynote, I tell them that I want to do more than just deliver excellent material on stage to get a standing ovation. It's not about me. I want to create an experience for those in attendance that's part of the over-all experience and that supports the objectives of the company. It's not about just having their people show up and listen to an agenda. It's about giving them the opportunity to have breakfast meetings with the speakers, make networking connections, and interchange ideas with each other, plus all the things that happen on the stage. Those are the kinds of things that create the emotion we're talking about.

When done properly, events bring certain dynamics to an or-ganization that can't be accomplished any other way. With one very important component—the emotional connection, which includes relationships and belief—they bring focus to the many aspects of *Strategic Mindset*, clarity, focus, and execution, all at once.

When most people think of events, they only think of a con-ference that's held in a hotel; and yet that's just one among the top five types of network marketing events:

1.   Conference calls (your weekly team call)

2.   Live broadcasts (Facebook, Zoom, and Skype)

3.   Home/office events (usually one to two hours, max)

4.   Hotel events: local, two to four hours; regional, five to eight hours; and national, two to four days

5.   Leadership retreats and reward trips

Each of these types of events can have an entirely different fo-cus. It could be basic training on sponsoring, launching, etc., or it could be for reward, motivation, or inspiration. However, each type of event must be thought through with the proper event mindsets:

☐ **Event Mindset No. 1:** This may be the only chance I ever get in front of this group; what is the best thing I can possibly do with the time allotted?

☐ **Event Mindset No 2:** How many ways can I involve people? Their participation will make the event more exciting, and it will be promoted better.

☐ **Event Mindset No. 3:** People won't usually remember most of what they hear at an event; they will, however, remember 100 percent of how they felt at the event.

The truth is, you can plan a three-day event and the majority of the people will only remember two or three things from the entire three days; and yet they'll absolutely remember how they felt about that event, and they'll talk about it for the next ten or twenty years if it was the right kind of experience. And even with just remembering a few things they learned, the next time you do it they will tell everyone in their group, "Hey, you have to be there. It's incredible!" And that applies to all five event types we listed above, even your conference calls. If people are only going to remember two or three things you say, then as a strategic networker you must

> **Event cycle:** Events create a unification, or a rallying-cry type of focus, for your organization. Without a proper event cycle laid out, you will be lacking major focus within your team.

give considerable thought to what those two or three things should be and how you are going to make them feel about them.

Each event must be strategically thought through. When you're coordinating an event, you're organizing multiple aspects. If you're going to be a strategic network marketer—if you're going to take your income from $50,000 or $100,000 up—you have to figure out how to either build a team to handle all of these aspects or hire someone to do it. Trying to do it yourself is simply not scalable.

Your Event Cycle

For most things in life, there's a cycle. Events are no different; and if you want to create momentum within your organization you'll want to adopt a strong, predictable event cycle for your team. This repetitive cycle gives strength to your organization, because it creates a rhythm in how things are perceived and how they get done. Events also create a unification, or a rallying-cry type of focus, for your organization. Without a proper event cycle laid out, you will be lacking major focus within your team. A proper event schedule should include a rhythm or a cycle of events.

Here's an example of a proper event cycle:

☐ **Month One:** Conference calls, a live broadcast, and local events (which include weekly in-home meetings and public hotel meetings, plus a monthly training)

☐ **Month Two:** Conference calls, a live broadcast, local events, and a *mini* regional event. (A mini regional event would pull from about a two-hour radius and would include training as well as opportunities to bring guests for an overview. This is usually conducted by someone with more experience, and the number of participants is usually over fifty and often into the hundreds.)

☐ **Month Three:** Conference calls, a live broadcast, local events, and a full regional event. (A full regional event would pull from about a six-hour radius, minimum, and would include one full day of training, inspiration, and motivation. More than likely, a speaker would be flown in, and there would be ample time to hear from top leaders. The number of participants is more than likely in the hundreds or thousands.)

This cycle should never stop. Generally, there are only three additional events that would take place each year:

1. Once or twice each year there should be a national event where the entire company comes together for corporate announcements, motivation, and training. There would be no full regional event that month.

2. Once or twice each year there may be a leadership retreat for those who have earned it.

3. Once each year there may be a *reward* trip for those who qualify (a cruise, a trip to an island, etc.).

Your Promotion Strategy

As a strategic networker, you should have a general outline of your year in advance; however, *you must have* a constant stream of events scheduled and being promoted for at least a minimum of ninety days out to maximize your team's effectiveness. Your promotion strategy for events must be very intentional and should include several facets.

In our world today, many network marketers rely too much on posting in social media and/or emailing. Although those two tools are very helpful, they're only two facets of a great promotional strategy. Your strategy should include several other facets to be fully effective:

1. **Numbers Goal.** When you're launching an event promotion, you should come up with a goal for the number of participants. Let's say your number is a hundred. Then your next step would be to identify the five people who could each influence twenty or more to come to the event. Once you've identified your five, you need to have a conversation with each one, explaining your expectations and outlining a plan for how they can influence their twenty. You should be sure to recommend that they physically call everyone

they possibly can, all the way down to the next leader. As a strategic networker, this is something you will have to help drive. And yes, that means you have to have actual conversations with actual people.

2. **Email.** An email strategy should then be implemented to highlight all the reasons people should be excited to come to the event. You should send at least one email each week to everyone you want to attend. Pricing, deadlines, and all other logistical information should be included in each email.

3. **Conference Calls.** It's healthy to bake in promotion (building up the event) in all conference calls within a certain period of time before each event. (That period will be longer, of course, for regional and national events.) Having guest speakers on to help promote, as well as strategically planning a specific call or two to allow your team to drive numbers, will go a long way toward helping to get the word out.

4. **Social Media.** You and several of your leaders should post promotions on social media several times a week. You may want to shoot quick videos to post, promote deadlines, and tease by mentioning a few exciting things that will happen at the event.

5. **The Next Event.** This works directly with your event cycle. There may be no better strategy for launching the promotion of events than doing it from another event, while you have everyone in the room and they are already excited. At every full regional event, you should always launch the next ninety days of events leading up to the next full regional or national event. You should have tickets ready for purchase three months out for full regional or national events, and at least one month out for mini regionals.

In most cases, you can't promote enough; however, it should be done in a way that feels right with everything else you are doing. Your goal as a leader is not to *shame* people into going to an event. (Unfortunately, that's a common mistake.) One of your key strategies should be to *inspire* them by communicating what's in it for them.

As a strategic network-marketing leader, you'll want to work with your leaders as your team grows to help them develop their own event strategies. Here are some things you'll want to remember:

1. Any one leader can really only pull in about fifty to a hundred people by themselves. If a leader says they'll bring two hundred people, then you'll want to ask them to show you who the five people are who will be bringing forty each.

2. You should never be shocked by the number of people who attended or did not attend your events. If you are, then you probably didn't communicate enough with your key leaders, or you didn't have an effective registration process.

3. Based on the number of people you expect to attend, you should always prepare in a way that makes your room look full, by adding tables and/or chairs or taking them out. At your local events, it's okay to have standing room only. Of course, at regional and national events you'll have a more accurate count, because most people will register in advance.

4. You'll want to write the agenda for your event no less than two weeks out (and it's best if you do it four or even eight weeks out). This gives your people time to digest the information, and you don't leave your leaders wondering what's going to happen.

5. The more you include your team members in the leadership of your events, the more ownership they'll take. Include them in decorations, printing, setup and breakdown,

brainstorming, and conference calls, and even let them help write the agenda. Just be sure you're listening to your highest performers and not just the loudest leaders.

Here's the bottom line: You want to know you haven't left any stone unturned. As long as you and your team promote as hard as you can, then whatever the numbers are, they are. Go to work with those who show up!

As a strategic network-marketing leader, you'll be able to create the force-multiplier effect at your events by doing these things:

1. Set the location and atmosphere of the event to be exciting, including decorations and the right music (high–energy, with meaning).

2. Build in recognition for promotions and new ranks, and make sure you don't overly rush through this. This is a force multiplier for belief. Seeing others achieve results tells those in the audience that they can do it, too. Just be careful to not keep recognizing the same people for the same thing.

3. Train on skills and character. When you're speaking to a crowd, address issues in a way that doesn't offend anyone. This multiplies your effectiveness, because it allows people to receive your instruction willingly. However, don't publicly address strong situations if they apply to only one or two in an audience of a hundred. Deal with those one-on-one.

4. Use stories to inspire belief. There is nothing more powerful than hearing someone else's story of struggle and victory. That's why you can often accomplish more in the area of belief in a two-hour seminar than you can in a hundred hours of counseling.

5. Effectively maximize training, announcements, and launching of promotions. The ultimate force multiplier is having your entire team in a room so you can train, announce,

and launch promotions with everyone experiencing and hearing the same message. Yes, you can do this on calls; however, when you add the physical experience of seeing, hearing, and feeling the excitement, you have a multiplier effect that can't be matched elsewhere.

Why Events?

Before we leave this topic, let's revisit the question of why events are so important for your organization. The emotional impact associated with events is a huge force multiplier. This industry is built on relationships; they're really what hold an organization together, and events are the primary strategy for cultivating new and existing relationships.

Everyone wants to be part of something larger than themselves. Events are where people start to solidify relationships with their team members—they share the excitement together, they share the dream together, and they make happy memories together. They begin to feel like they've become part of a larger family—a family that has aspirations similar to their own—and it gives them a feeling of belonging. They hear the stories and testimonies of others who have done what they want to do, and they're energized. They rub shoulders with people who have built large organizations, and the personal contact makes it more real for them. There's really no other strategy that comes close to building relationships in such a dynamic way.

Now let's talk about another very powerful force multiplier for your network-marketing business—tools.

Tools

Strategy No. 14 VIP: Tools create the leverage that ultimately creates your freedom!

Tools will make you rich! I'm not referring to selling them—I'm referring to using them. They are major force multipliers for your network-marketing business, because they give you many wins. A strategic networker thinks about tools differently than the average distributor. They realize that if their teams are using tools, their businesses will grow faster.

I (Tony) developed a whole video series for the network-marketing industry called *Tools Work,* and the main message of the series is that tools give you leverage. They can go where you can't go, they can stay longer than you can stay, and they can be more perfect in messaging than you can be.

Many people don't understand how to get their teams to take on the responsibility of using tools consistently. And it is a responsibility! Often distributors don't treat their business like a real business. They simply rely on their upline to supply tools for them and their teams. *After all*, they think, *my upline is already making money. They can afford it.* How far would the conventional business owner get if they chose not to invest in the basic tools they would need and instead sit around and wait on magical growth to happen?

(Note: The only exception to this is when you or someone above you is driving depth. At that point, you will be investing into their business. But guess what! You're the one that's building the respect and the leadership. In essence, you're driving *your* business, not theirs—they just get the benefit.)

Tools versus Skills

Tools often take a back seat to skills, which dismantles what I (Ryan) call the "relatability factor." The relatability factor is your ability to use your developed skillset while building and maintaining a belief within your prospect that says, I can do what this person is doing. As a strategic networker, it's important to understand and embrace this concept, and then help your leaders embrace it.

Let me explain. As time goes on, your competence as a network marketer goes up, and so do your presentation and delivery skills. That's really great—at least until you get so good that the new person across the table from you is thinking, I'll never be able to *be that good.*

One sure fire way for this to happen is when great presenters don't use tools. Let's say your company has a video about your products, and yet you or your team leaders constantly feel the need to present the products yourself, without using the video. That's a time when skillset can actually cause momentum to slow down instead of speed up. As a leader, you must remember that the new prospect is evaluating whether or not they can do what you're doing. So if you want to relate to the masses, you will use tools. Now this doesn't mean that your skillsets should go without being used. They just should be used around the tools and not instead of them. When you use your skillset around tools, you maximize the tool without sacrificing the relatability factor. Your prospect sees you using something they can use (a tool); and because your skillset supports the information presented in the tool instead of replacing it altogether, you're relatable. And at the same time, you're *effective.*

I (Tony) use and promote tools in a huge way within my own business and with every client I have. I will often ask someone, "How's your tool box?" What I'm really asking is what kind of tools they have in their vehicle, their briefcase, or their backpack.

Most people don't have a system for keeping their tools accessible in those places. In all of my vehicles—my Sprinter RESULTS1 van, my Mercedes SLS, and my Navigator—I have a box that contains my brochures, my business cards, some of my books and videos, and a variety of other things, so I'm always prepared. I'll often suggest to my network marketing clients, "Let's go look in your car and in your back pack. Then let's look at the things you could have around you to make sure you have a great tool box ready to go. This is a duplication business and you want people looking to you as a leader, so you need to make sure you're leveraging a great tool box. And if the company is spending thousands of dollars—sometimes tens or hundreds of thousands of dollars—building the best tools for you, don't you, as a leader, want your team to duplicate having a box full of those tools ready to go? Then, instead of saying to a prospect or someone on your team, 'I'll mail that to you later,' you would be able to say, 'I'll go out to the car and get it for you right now.' That's something that can make a powerful difference in your business." (It's always good to teach this to others and to make sure you model it yourself.)

One quick way, then, to tell if someone is serious about their network-marketing business (becoming a strategic networker) is to look in the trunk of their car. They're either equipped or they're not; they're either expecting success or they're not. Many people can get their income up to $30,000 to $50,000 a year just off of skillset; however, they often don't realize that their lack of tool mentality can be a real obstacle to the growth of their organization. They're frustrated because they're not duplicating fast, and yet they don't have any tools in the trunk of their car. They're simply not expecting growth.

I (Ryan) am reminded of the story of the church that was in the middle of a long Texas drought. The area in which they lived hadn't had rain for about three months, when the pastor said, "Let's have an outdoor picnic and pray for rain." The afternoon of the picnic and prayer meeting came, and they had a great time of prayer and fellowship. During the festivities, however, the pastor couldn't help but notice a little girl holding an umbrella. Since it was so hot and dry, he walked over to the little girl and asked her why she was holding an umbrella. Her answer was, "Well, Pastor, I knew we were coming to pray for rain, so I wanted to be prepared." Everyone else had come to pray for rain; the little girl came expecting it! Are you prepared for and expecting your business to explode into momentum?

Without tools, each person must come up with a way to share inspiring and accurate information about the products and the opportunity—reinventing the wheel, so to speak. And without tools, building your business can become a time-consuming process filled with frustration, disappointment, and defeat. Without tools there can really be no expectation for rain (momentum).

These are the network-marketing tools you should have in ample supply:

☐ Applications (hard copy or online access by phone or in your phone)

☐ Launching (new member) materials

☐ Product brochures (hard copy or electronic)

☐ Basic training audios/videos

☐ Presentation videos (or organized links)

☐ Flipcharts and markers

☐ Sample products

In addition to business-building tools, it's a good idea to have a few extra leadership and network-marketing books and audios available. Jim Rohn's *How to Build Your Network Marketing Business* is a great audio to always have on hand.

You should have enough of your business materials on hand to be able to *sell* (yes, *sell*) to new members when they join, in order to launch their new business. Although you might give a few to your personally sponsored people, it's not your job to run a charity. Many have a hard time asking people to buy tools after they join, and this sets a non-business tone for your new members from the very beginning. Don't try to oversell the amount they need, of course; however, don't hesitate to sell them everything they need to launch their business if they are serious about building it. You want to sell the concept of investing to grow faster.

Here's a great idea: Get out your tool order form and highlight everything you absolutely need to move someone from A to Z within your system. Then organize a pack of these tools, if your company hasn't already, and have them ready for new members to access in quantities.

When tools get updated, people often hesitate to buy the new tools because they have a hard time throwing away their old ones. In reality, if they had built their business consistently, they shouldn't have many, if any, tools left to throw away. Just so you'll know, when you are aggressively in the middle of a ninety-day run, you *will* run out of tools! Period! And again, this is a business. If McDonald's changes the branding on a particular item, their franchisees throw away the old and bring in the new. It's simply a part of business and a part of marketing. Understand that you will make a lot of money when you use the tools the right way.

In reality, the best way to create a tools culture is to constantly promote them; more importantly, though, let your team see you *all in* when it comes to tools. Here are some guidelines to help you create a tools culture:

1. Lead by example. Let your team see you open up your trunk to a full box of tools.

2. Work to have a tool that answers almost every question anyone could ask (product tools, how-to-build tools, presentation tools, etc.).

3. Don't try to invent your own tools (there are a few exceptions). Use as many company-developed tools as possible, because that proves that you're a team player and that *you follow a system*. (That means you cannot create a team-specific tool to replace company tools. In other words, use the company's tools unless you need a tool the company hasn't created. And if you really do need to create your own, make sure it reinforces any related tools the company has developed. If the company has a presentation video, for example, don't create another one just because you want to be in it.)

4. Have plenty of tools at your local events and teach regularly on best practices involving tools and how to use them.

Six Compelling Reasons for Creating a Tools Culture:

1. Tools really are the only way you *won't* have to be somewhere all the time.

2. If you want 1,000 people presenting the *same* thing the *same* way, you must have a tool they can use.

3. If you want 1,000 people saying the *same* thing about a given product, you must have a tool they can use.

4. If you want to attract non-sales-type people by the thousands, you must have tools.

5. If you want to keep it simple and duplicate *fast,* you must have tools.

6. The right tools are really what makes it possible to have the *lifestyle* and *residual income* you want in network marketing.

In network marketing, the goal is to get a lot of people doing the same thing over and over again. What you might not quite understand is, there's only one proven way in this industry to get 1,000 people saying the same thing, and that's with a tool. There's only one way you can get 1,000 people presenting the same presentation, and that's with a tool. Any other strategy outside of that (and there will be many variations) will not synergistically duplicate. If you do anything that doesn't have a tool attached to it, you are purposely sabotaging your ability to grow an organization of 1,000 people.

You'll want to keep an eye out (focus) to make sure the tool mindset is duplicating within your group. As you are working downline or attending larger meetings, see whether there are tools at the back table, and take note at the end of the meetings to see whether people are handing prospects a tool for follow-up.

> **Tools Culture:** In network marketing, there's only one proven way to get 1,000 people saying the same thing and presenting the same presentation, and that's with tools.

Strategically help educate your team on a regular basis until someone else on your team takes up this responsibility. You'll know you have an upcoming leader when you see them take on the tools leadership role for their team.

Now let's look at another powerful force multiplier for your network-marketing business—recognition.

Recognition

Strategy No 15 VIP: People will do more for
a twenty-five-cent ribbon (recognition)
than they will for a $1,000 check.

I (Ryan) have seen that what gets people excited may be the life-style and the money, what gets them emotionally committed is their "why," and what drives them to perform is usually recognition. Recognition is a powerful tool.

Something I say quite often to my leaders when we're discussing recognition and creating momentum is, "People will do more for a twenty-five-cent ribbon than they will for a $1,000 check." Now, I'm not saying they don't want the $1,000 check; however, a person's desire to be recognized and feel significant is so important in life, and when we can fill that need it becomes a very powerful tool that will motivate them to build their business more than just about anything else.

Now, understand that it needs to be done the right way; we should never manipulate people. And yet we have to know that if we tell them, "If you do ten presentations this month, you'll get to walk the stage and be recognized in front of 500 people," they'll be much more likely to do it than if we say, "I'll give you a $200 check for doing ten presentations." That's just not going to move them the same way. And there's a reason for that...

Maslow's Hierarchy of Needs

I (Tony) have recognized, studied, and taught for years Maslow's Hierarchy of Needs, which basically substantiates the fact that we all have a powerful need for recognition.

At the bottom of the pyramid are physiological needs; at the very minimum, we have to survive by eating. Once we can eat, then we have to worry about not getting shot, destroyed, kidnapped, mugged, or injured, and that goes for our family, as well. You eat first, then take care of safety. Then the third need is that we

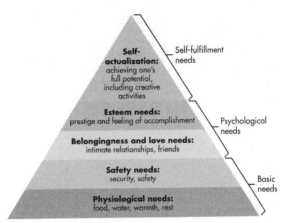

crave belonging, or being loved. That's where the network-marketing business starts kicking in. The sense of belonging is a massive deal in network marketing. People want to belong to the company, and they want even more to belong to a local team. They want to feel valued, needed, and wanted, and that they have a chance—that they're able to grow and reach their potential, which is the fourth level, the need for esteem. When they get on the stage and are recognized at an event, their esteem starts kicking in and they think, *Look what I did. I feel good about myself.* That's where recognition really starts touching their needs.

And at the highest level, you get to what I often call "Yoda." When I fly in to deliver a keynote and I get to help people be their best, then I'm at my fifth level, which is self-actualization; I'm now feeling good about myself because I'm able to tap my thinking into other people.

People crave the top three levels, and network marketing applies heavily to levels three and four. So what that says is that you, as a leader, should strategically learn how to run promotions within your organization so you can create the right opportunities for recognition within your own team, in addition to whatever the company does.

Recognition versus Edification

One of the most important things you need to know is the difference between recognition and edification. There's a big difference.

To edify means "to instruct or benefit, especially morally or spiritually; uplift."[9]

When you edify someone, it means that you hold them up in a way that tells your team, "This is who you need to be like."

> **Edification versus Recognition:** When you edify someone, it means that you hold them up in a way that tells your team, "This is who you need to be like." When you recognize someone, it's usually for something they have achieved—a goal.

When you recognize someone, it's usually for something they have achieved—a goal.

Edification is much more sacred and should be treated as such. For example, if someone joins your team and builds a fast business in their first thirty days, you should recognize them and not edify them. They simply haven't earned the credibility to be edified. If you tell your team that this is the person they should

---

9   Dictionary.com, s.v. "edify," accessed May 23, 2017, http:\\www.dictionary.com\browse\edify.

all be like, what do you say when that person quits the next month and you find out they've done the same thing in five other companies—built for a month and then left? If you have edified them, guess what? Some of your team will go with them.

Edification should be earned over time, much like credibility. You should be extremely careful who you allow to speak to your team regarding their habits, lifestyle, and leadership. It's perfectly fine to allow new people to teach on topics they're excelling in; just be careful not to over-endorse newer people who haven't yet earned it. Your people are judging your ability as a leader to select the right people to guide them and speak into their lives. If you select the wrong people too many times, it will come back to bite you.

> " **Earned Edification:** Edification should be earned over time, much like credibility. Your people are judging your ability as a leader to select the right people to guide them and speak into their lives. If you select the wrong people too many times, it will come back to bite you. "

When you edify something (or someone), it's understood that you endorse it as being in alignment with your values system. Now, think about that. You have to be extremely careful, because what you edify is going to be duplicated and will create behavior patterns within your organization. That means if you praise people for some things that are not in harmony with what you want, you're going to get the wrong behavior, over time, from your organization. You either edify solid principles or you edify hype—you choose.

So how do you know who to select for edification? Look at their:

1. Values: Are their values in alignment with someone you would want to endorse? If not, then it will come across as fake, and people will think you're only edifying to make money.

2. Trustworthiness: Does the team *trust* this person? Trust can sometimes take time; if the person you're edifying is doing well in the business and yet in way that's not trustworthy, it will come back to bite you.

3. Skills: Does this person possess the skillset you want everyone to model? If not, let them grow a little before you edify. Simply recognize them until they show themselves worthy of edification.

If your team sees you on stage edifying someone they know is not of the right character just because they made some money, they will begin to question your integrity as a leader. They would likely wonder if you're not being truthful about other things, since you're saying something about that person they know is not true. This industry is built on belief and trust, and if you lie or stretch the truth or say something that's not congruent with those values, then you lose credibility.

One of the biggest confusion points surrounding recognition is "What should we recognize?" Too many people recognize intentions rather than achievement.

People often introduce someone to me and they say, "Hey, Ryan, I want you to meet my new member, John." (Please don't say "my new member" like you own them!J) "John has just joined, and he's going to hit [a certain] rank in the next four weeks!" Usually John has a puzzled look on his face when he's introduced to me this way, because he's not even made the first phone call! People think they're making John feel good when they do this. They're not! What they're doing is actually setting the wrong tone for him. In fact, he's almost doomed from the beginning. Why? Because he hasn't done anything yet, the people around him have been working hard and aren't getting recognized, and now there may be an improper expectation placed on him that he's not ready to live up to. The easiest thing for John to do is quit. Most people quit our industry for one of two or three reasons, and one is because they think they've failed or they didn't live up to what was set out for them.

> **What to Recognize:** Too many people recognize intentions rather than achievement. Most people quit our industry for one of two or three reasons, and one is because they think they've failed or they didn't live up to what was set out for them.

A better introduction would be, "Hey, Ryan, meet my friend John. He just joined the team and is looking forward to getting started. Are there any tips you can give him?" This positions John in a way that he still feels like he needs to get started (if he hasn't) and not feel like he needs to prove something. That simple principle is often the difference between getting people to perform because of recognition and causing them to stagnate because of improper recognition.

When John has set ten appointments, made presentations to five people, and signed up two new distributors, and then you recognize him for his results, several things will likely happen. He will begin to psychologically connect with the proper behaviors that get publicly rewarded. Since everyone wants to feel important, he will likely strive to repeat his actions. In addition, you end up sending the right signals to your team as to what they need to do to get recognized.

You need to recognize for:

1. Personal sponsoring

2. Customer gathering

3. Rank achievement

4. Promotion qualification

5. Exhibiting the behaviors you want modeled

Do not recognize for:

1. Intentions

2. Goals (that haven't been achieved)

3. Past careers

4. A person's conventional success as if it's network marketing success

5. Exhibiting the behaviors you do not want modeled

As a rule of thumb, someone should usually be a part of an organization and be performing at a high level for six to twelve months before you cross over to edification. Let them prove themselves. Remember, you don't really know who someone is until something isn't going their way.

Once you learn and understand these principles, then you can strategically recognize and edify to build the proper team and company culture.

You see, now, how events, tools, and recognition can be huge force multipliers for your network-marketing business. Remember, the more habits/systems you can create and the more automatic you become, the less you have to use the cerebral cortex part of your brain for menial tasks and the more you can use it for the things you're learning in this book, like focusing on HLAs. In the case of events, for example, creating a habit/system for automatically putting the company's schedule of events on your calendar would move that task into the basal ganglia. If you automatically put the company's best tools into your vehicles and backpack as they become available, that becomes a way of operation and frees your brain for other things that need more thought. And creating a system for automatically recognizing people for their achievements would ensure no one falls through the cracks and free your mind up to focus on other leadership strategies.

In the next chapter, we'll look at three of those leadership strategies: accountability, communication, and trust.

VIPs

- [ ] Force Multiplier: A force multiplier is a factor that dramatically increases (multiplies) the effectiveness—and thus the results—of something you're doing.

- [ ] Events: People won't usually remember most of what they hear at an event; they will, however, remember 100 percent of how they felt at the event.

- [ ] The Why: The "why" that comes from events is an emotional connection that solidifies the relationship people have with the company and with their team, and it can only be accomplished through events.

- [ ] Event cycle: Events create a unification, or a rallying-cry type of focus, for your organization. Without a proper event cycle laid out, you will be lacking major focus within your team.

- [ ] Tools: Tools create the leverage that ultimately creates your freedom!

- [ ] Tools Culture: In network marketing, there's only one proven way to get 1,000 people saying the same thing and presenting the same presentation, and that's with tools.

- [ ] Recognition: People will do more for a twenty-five-cent ribbon (recognition) than they will for a $1,000 check.

- [ ] Edification versus Recognition: When you edify someone, it means that you hold them up in a way that tells your team, "This is who you need to be like." When you recognize someone, it is usually for something they have achieved—a goal.

- [ ] Earned Edification: Edification should be earned over time, much like credibility. Your people are judging your ability as a leader to select the right people to guide them and speak into their lives. If you select the wrong people too many times, it will come back to bite you.

☐ What to Recognize: Too many people recognize intentions rather than achievement. Most people quit our industry for one of two or three reasons, and one is because they think they've failed or they didn't live up to what was set out for them.

Self-Evaluation

On a scale of 1 to 5, with 5 being the highest, rate yourself on the five issues below to determine where you are in effectively using the force multipliers of events, tools, and recognition to grow your business.

1. I have adopted the three proper event mindsets and consistently maximize them when conducting the five event types in my network-marketing business.

2. I have scheduled events for my organization a year in advance, and I utilize a proper and effective promotion strategy so that I get maximum participation for each event.

3. I create exciting events for my people and give them a great experience that stimulates an emotional connection with their "why."

4. I have created a tools culture in my business, and I set the example by both maintaining a proper toolbox and using tools for maximum effectiveness.

5. I understand the need for belonging and esteem, so I put great emphasis on properly recognizing the people on my team and I only edify people after they've earned it.

Chapter Six

Leadership

Now that you're armed with the *Strategic Mindset* that it takes to climb to the highest levels in this business, the clarity and focus you need to take your execution all the way to the top, and three powerful force multipliers that will significantly enhance your efforts, let's see how it all plays out in taking your leadership to the next level.

Here's our definition of leadership, as it applies to network marketing: A leader is one who can inspire people through example to positively do things they otherwise wouldn't do to reach their potential.

Leadership is really more about principles and integrity than tactics. And because principles and integrity can be learned, they are also skills; however, they must be honed into instincts over time.

The result of true leadership is influence, which has little to do with position or title. As a strategic networker, you must understand that when people refer to you as a bad, good, or great leader, they are more often than not referring to your character skills rather than your technical skills. In other words, the business-building skillset is one of the smaller components of leadership. With this in mind, let me (Ryan) tell you something that may surprise you: *There is really no training out there on how to be a better leader.* For example, one of the best-selling leadership books of all time, *Developing the Leader Within You,* by Dr. John Maxwell, has not one chapter on the skillset of leadership. What it does have, however, is a chapter on attitude, a chapter on relationships, a chapter on priorities, etc. When you are intentional about mastering these areas of your life, and when you bring them into your network-marketing business, you can't help but become a leader—even a *High Performing Leader.*

A *High Performing Leader* Creates a *High Performing Team*

You may remember the story we told in chapter four about how Ford paid me (Tony) a million dollars in the early 90s to bring their top leaders into a team-building synergistic state. I immediately jumped in and started studying all of the distinctions about team building. I poured a year of my life into understanding the difference between a group and a team, and I learned how to bring people together into a *High Performing Team.* Since that time I've proved it out over and over and positively impacted many organizations (including many network-marketing organizations) with this expertise, and I'm going to share it with you now.

Let me start out by giving you the incredible benefits of leveraging team synergy:

☐ It uses collective intelligence and expertise. Let me give you an example: When we were in my studio last year recording the videos for my *RESULTS Faster!* online video course and accompanying book, we had about fifteen people supporting us to make that special experience for our viewers, and we were tapping everyone's years of expertise as a team to bring it all together. The result was a powerful course and book that will help people all over the world accelerate their results. (Visit tonyjeary.com/resultsfaster-webinar.) It was a beautiful experience to watch the team's synergy bring the best of my life's work together and make it happen.

☐   It expands leadership. Team synergy allows you to mentor people more and bring them up as leaders.

☐   It promotes fantastic team engagement and enjoyment. We all feel good when we're part of a winning team.

☐   Execution is improved; hence, results happen. With team synergy, everyone benefits.

Now let's take a look at the characteristics of a *High Performing Team*, and then we're going to give you the three very best things you can do as a leader to make a *High Performing Team* a reality for you.

In that year of studying the distinctions of a *High Performing Team*, we created a model that explains the difference between a group, a team, and a *High Performing Team*. As we look at this model, think about your own network-marketing organization, wheth-er you have six people or six hundred, and re-member that you, as the leader, are the one who determines whether your organization will be a *High Performing Team*. Your people will follow your lead.

Level one in the model is the group. In a group, the people work with no common goals, and each person works

> **"**
>
> **High Performing Team:** A *High Performing Team* works together to get the very best results, and they continually reevaluate to make sure they produce the best quality.
>
> **"**

independently. They may do fairly well on their own or in their own groups and be able to make things happen to a point, and yet they really aren't synergized. You add it all up, and there can still be wins. Many organizations function at this level, where their people are in groups and not really part of a team.

Level two is the team. It's a group of people working together interdependently toward a common goal. A team is one level above a group, and yet it still is not the top level.

Where you really want to be is level three, and that's operating as a *High Performing Team*. At this level, your people are focused on being as effective as possible. They work together to get the very best results, and they continually reevaluate to make sure they produce the best quality. Each team member has a high level of investment in the outcomes, so each individual is highly motivated. That's a *High Performing Team*. Don't get stuck in leading a group, or even a team. Take it to the highest level—a *High Performing Team*.

> **High Performing Leader:** When you truly hold yourself accountable, employ proper communication, and are trusted by your followers, then and only then will you be known as a *High Performing Leader* (HPL).

So now you want to be at that level, and you're saying, "How do I make that happen?" Both Ryan and I have been working in a high-level leadership capacity for more than fifty years, combined, so when I introduced Ryan almost a decade ago to the three crossover strategies that make the difference in moving up through the levels of team performance, he immediately adopted them into network marketing. This system of building a *High Performing Team* is based on intentionally implementing three strategies: Accountability, Communication, and Trust (A.C.T). When you truly hold yourself accountable, employ proper communication, and are trusted by your followers, then and only then will you be known as a *High Performing Leader* (HPL). Let's take a look at each of those three strategies.

Strategic Networker Strategy No. 16

Accountablility

Strategy No 16 VIP: The leadership side of accountability is far more effective than the management side of accountability.

Leadership verses Management

There's a difference between leadership and management, and as a *High Performing Leader* (HPL), you need to understand the difference. Leadership is inspiring your team and showing them direction. Management can be similar to babysitting them to make sure they're doing what they say they're going to do. Both are important, and yet both need to be completely understood. When you manage, you have to follow up, double check, and really stay on top of your people for accountability. You will almost always need to manage some. With others, though, you will lead by casting the vision of the results you (or they) are looking for, and they take them and run with them. You set the example, inspire, motivate, and encourage, and then they come back and tell you what they've accomplished. You don't have to watch their every step to get it done.

When someone comes into your world as part of your team, you have to size them up at the beginning and decide, *Am I going to have to manage them a little bit more, or am I going to be able to lead them?* You can often determine that from their personality style (which we'll talk about later in this chapter). Using the DISC Personality Profile, if a person's natural personality is a "C," they will usually hold themselves to a high level of accountability. A person who

> **Leadership versus Management:** Leadership is inspiring your team and showing them direction. Management can be similar to babysitting them to make sure they're doing what they say they're going to do.

is an "I" is very outgoing and social and may sometimes forget what they promised, so they may need a little more management in the beginning.

A huge mistake I (Ryan) see leaders making within our industry is when they think, *Okay, I'm going to hold this person accountable.* What they're really thinking is, *I'm going to manage this person to perform at a higher level.* It doesn't work that way. Most people lean too hard on the management side of accountability and fail to see how effective the leadership side is.

Leading By Relationships

It's great to organize groups to have an accountability conference call; and yet the reality is, those individuals don't turn into *High Performing Teams* unless you're rolling up your sleeves and building relationships with them.

I believe a big part of what drives the performance of your people is the relationship they have with someone they trust—someone they want to be proud of them. I'll confess right up front that one of the things that has driven me for years is seeking approval from Tony—as well as a few others—because I respect him, I trust him, and I view him as a mentor. Because of our relationship, I hold myself accountable to him. Early on in my network-marketing career it was my upline; I found someone I really respected. They didn't have to call me to motivate me. I was in constant communication with them, because I wanted them to be proud of what

I was doing; therefore, I took very seriously the conversations we had and sought to perform so I would get their approval.

I believe a leader in network marketing is successful only when they're able to establish that kind of accountability with their people. Remember that we said leadership is inspiring your people and showing them direction; in network marketing, especially, that's accomplished through building relationships with your people.

As a leader, you have to be intentional about accountability. You can't just hope your people will become accountable. You have to *intentionally* create a culture of accountability by making sure to set in motion the things we've discussed.

Who Holds the Leader Accountable?

We've talked about holding your people accountable; however, who holds you, as a leader, accountable? Actually, there are three answers to that question:

1. Yourself. I (Ryan) recently came across this quote by John Adams, the second president of the United States: "Although we can't predict the total success we will have in our future, we can make sure that we deserve it." In other words, we need to make sure we lead ourselves well.

2. A mentor. This may be the person who brought you into the business or someone above them in your upline, who is pouring into you what you should pour into others.

3. A coach. This is someone you pay, generally on the outside of your business, who will mentor you, hold you accountable, and bring strength to you.

The truth is, you will be ineffective in holding your people accountable to grow personally if you're not in an aggressive personal-development plan yourself. And you will be ineffective as a network-marketing leader in getting your people to properly fill their calendars if you're not intentionally filling your calendar with the right things. And the right things are the five network marketing HLA's we laid out in chapter three:

1. **Sponsoring (dream building):** Since this is the number one thing you can do (helping people connect their dreams with what you're doing) at all levels in your business, it should be a staple on your calendar.

2. **Launching (starting new members):** Outside of sponsoring, this is the number one HLA that fuels everything in your organization and keeps the momentum going.

3. **Driving Depth:** Working with your team to lead you to someone to work with who will lead you to someone who will lead you to someone is possibly the single most strategic HLA you can do.

4. **Promoting (numbers at events):** Make sure proper promotion is baked in to what you're doing on a daily basis.

5. **Training (personal, leadership, and business development):** If you really want to keep your team moving along, you'll train them on a systematic basis.

All five HLAs require non-stop action if you want to be a *High Performing Leader* who sets the example for your team; your calendar will reflect whether you're serious about that goal.

The bottom line is that leadership is intentional, and it's only the intentional leaders who build big teams that last.

Communication

Strategy No. 17 VIP: Intentional communication (understanding the who, what, how, how much, and how often) categorizes your level of leadership more effectively than any other skill in your arsenal.

Communication is one of the most exciting and yet frustrating strategies for any leader. This section is designed to offer insight and instruction on how to think, act, and be in such a way that allows your personal style of communication to flourish. The principles outlined here can be adapted to any personality style, and they are principles you'll find in common with the most respected top earners in the industry.

Strategic networkers understand that the industry they've chosen is a very emotional one and therefore requires much consideration regarding some of the elements we'll teach in this section, which we call "communication maximizers." They include things such as using people skills, problem solving, strategies for communicating with your team, and the power of understanding personality profiles. Becoming a better communicator begins with an understanding of how important every interaction you have really is—especially in your network-marketing business.

Life is a Series of Presentations

I (Tony) authored a book a few years ago called *Life Is a Series of Presentations*, which was published by Simon and Schuster, and I was fortunate to get a great endorsement out of the blue from Daymond John with Shark Tank when he talked about this book as one of the six top all-time books anyone in business should read. It's one of my favorite best-sellers that I've ever published, because it really helps people understand the importance of intentional communication in every interaction.

> **Life is a Series of Presentations:** Life is a Series of Presentations. Every encounter you have, you're *presenting* yourself and you're representing yourself and/or your business.

Every encounter you have—whether it's with a prospect, a colleague, a friend, or your spouse—*you're presenting yourself,* and you're *representing yourself* and/or your business. In other words, the way you present your thoughts and ideas to people—whether it's to someone in your group, your leaders, your inner circle, or someone you're talking to about joining your network-marketing business—affects your brand, or how you are perceived. Your presentation really does make a difference. It can also have a profound impact in shaping someone's life, or it can be the key as to whether someone takes the right action to grow their business.

Presentation/communication, both personally and professionally, is more than a skillset. It's a strategic asset. The goal, then, perhaps should be to work toward mastery on the presentation impact curve, and here's how that works: Some people stay at the good level, some people move to great, and some people live in the mastery level where they see the greatest results. Ryan and I would like to help you move into mastery.

How effective are you in communicating? Whether you think you are at the level of good or great or mastery, we want to challenge you to think about these three things: *How well do you prepare? How well do you deliver? And how well do you follow up?*

Many leaders in network marketing fail to be intentional when it comes to communicating, and I (Ryan) believe it categorizes their level of leadership more effectively than any other skill. In other words, great communication skills brand you as a great leader and poor communication skills brand you as a poor leader quicker than just about anything else. Communication for the network-marketing leader should be for the purpose of motivation, inspiration, and/or instruction.

I (Ryan) have learned so much from Tony over the years about communication. In fact, when I read his *Life is a Series of Presentations* book years ago, it literally changed forever the way I present in front of a group. For example, before I read his book I thought nothing of having ten or fifteen points in my presentation. While reading the book, I realized that just presenting three or four major points well is far more effective and is really all your audience can absorb.

When it comes to preparing your communications to your network-marketing group, whether it's one-on-one, through email, or from the stage in front of a group, consider these things:

1. Who am I speaking to (who is my audience)?

2. What is my purpose for communicating (what are my objectives)?

3. What are the major points I want to communicate?

4. How am I going to make each point (verbally, with a video clip, using a flip chart, etc.)?

5. How much detail do I need to go into (how long will I spend on each point)?

Effective communication and presentation skills require you to plan what you want to say, and how you will *deliver* that message. Tony has created an excellent instrument to use in preparing your presentation/communication that is extremely helpful in determining the answers to those questions. It's called the 3-D Outline™.

3-D Outline™

This matrix will help you organize your thoughts and actions by giving you space to document information about your audience, objectives, key points, timing, and more. After you use it a few times, you'll see how you can customize it to fit your unique presentation needs. Whether you're presenting to one person or a large group, the 3-D Outline™ enables you to keep everything you need on track and in line.

3-D Outline™

Presentation Title:				Delivery Date:	
Audience:				Start Time:	
Objectives:				End Time:	
Final Preparation:	[ ] [ ]			[ ] [ ]	

#	Start Time	Length	What	Why	How	Who
1.						
2.						
3.						
4.						

Here's an example of how you may complete a 3–D Outline™ for structuring a network marketing presentation you're making at an event:

3–D Outline™

Presentation Title:	Company Visions and Opportunity Presentation			Delivery Date:	1/1/2020
Audience:	New and existing members. Catered to first-time guest.			Start Time:	7pm
Objectives:	Articulate the vision, purpose, and personal benefits; build belief; and present the financial opportunity			End Time:	8pm
Final Preparation:	[]		[]		
	[]		[]		

#	Start Time	Length	What	Why	How	Who
1.	7:00	10	Opening	Set the stage for what they will experience and high level overview	General speaking	Host of Event
2.	7:10	15	Opening Personal Story	To create belief and connection between audience and speaker.	General Speaking	Main Speaker
3.	7:25	20	Products, Purpose, and Plan	To create belief in all aspects of your company. To share the benefits of your product, to present a compelling purpose behind what you are doing, and to show the plan for your opportunity	PowerPoint/ Video	Main Speaker
4.	7:45	15	Testimonials and close of meeting	Build belief, and ask for the sale	Videos or live speakers Pass out applications and walk through process to become a customer or distributor	Satisfied customers and members. Main speaker to close with compelling reason

I PRESENT

The core content of Tony's book *Life is a Series of Presentations* is a list of eight strategic presentation/communication concepts that will help you be more intentional in all of your communication efforts, whether written or spoken, and whether to one person or a thousand. They're presented in the mnemonic I PRESENT:

I **I**nvolve the audience! One of the best ways to do this is ask questions or have people write things down. When they write things down they get engaged. (And here's another win: Their eyes go down, and you get a breathing space.) In almost every speech I (Tony) give, whether it's to two hundred people or twenty thousand people, I start with a question. Even when I get on the phone, I start with a question. So many times we talk too much, and we don't ask for enough involvement.

P **P**repare your audience. Many times in today's world we invite people to a meeting or another type of presentation, and we fail to list the rich benefits they'll get when they attend. And when you're presenting before a group, a great way to prepare your audience is to touch people before you talk. That involves going out and shaking hands with the members of your audience, whether it's ten people or two hundred or two thousand. Also, incorporate a strong Host Introduction, and then open with a solid payoff. The first thing you say really does matter. People start absorbing right away.

R **R**esearch and build a powerful presentation arsenal. Start with a mental arsenal of things you keep in your mind. Look around and build your arsenal with ideas you can save and use for the future. That includes things you can use in an electronic arsenal—with things you have in your phone, for example—and it includes hard copy and material props, like things you can give away.

E Explain the why! This is so powerful, but people miss it all the time! Make sure to give the why by using words like "because" and "so that." It's so important to do that in every presentation—even in an email! I might say, for example, "One of the things I encourage you to do is build a great arsenal so that you're more content rich when you need to give a presentation."

S State management. If you're giving a presentation to a group of ten or more, you will probably have all these states in your audience:

1. The vacationers—they're really not troublemakers; they're just vacationing when they are in front of you.

2. The prisoners—those who have their arms crossed and really don't want to be there

3. The graduates—the people who know it all

4. The students—the people who are really there to learn and absorb

A master presenter is continually moving people to the student mentality so they want to hear and learn what they have to say.

E Eliminating the unknowns. When we take every unknown to the known, then our confidence level goes up. When I (Tony) walk onto a stage before I give a presentation, I've already turned my unknowns into knowns. My team has already sent me pictures of the stage, my views from the stage, and the audience's views, so I don't have to worry about setup. And before the presentation, I look for every possible way I can pre-test the mic so I feel comfortable with the technical aspects. I even know things like when I am going to walk onto the stage to meet the person who is introducing me and when and where we're going to shake hands. Turning every unknown into a known allows you to be less nervous and more impactful!

N k**N**ow your audience! Create a mental profile of your audience members (whoever you're communicating with), which could include age, background, and education. When you're communicating with network-marketing groups, another question you will want to consider is how long the average person in the room has been in the industry or company. If 90 percent of the people in the room have been in less than ninety days, then your information should be slanted to appeal to that group. If 50 percent have been in for two years and 50 percent have been in two months, then you'll want to add some meat into your message so that everyone leaves getting something. It's important to understand your audience so you can target your objectives to meet their particular needs.

T **T**ailor your presentation! I developed a concept called *Planned Spontaneity,* which is being so prepared in advance that you can be flexible and ready to adjust your presentation to fit whatever issues may come up from your audience.

We encourage you to study these eight concepts and use them to help you take your presentations to the highest level.

Communication Maximizers

The following skills will allow you as a leader to maximize your results when communicating.

1. Using people skills in communication

    Great people skills are the key to great communication and thus great leadership. As a matter of fact, I (Ryan) consider people skills the number one skill a leader can possess. Think about it—almost all leadership problems can be traced back to something that was said or communicated that either shouldn't have been said at all or was said wrong.

Many of you have probably read *How to Win Friends and Influence People*, by Dale Carnegie, and you may have even talked about some of the concepts when you've communicated with your people. How many of those principles have you really understood and applied yourself, though, in your communication with your team? Principles like:

a. Don't criticize, condemn, or complain

b. Give honest and sincere appreciation

c. Become genuinely interested in other people

d. Smile

e. Show respect for the other person's opinions. Never say, "You're wrong."

f. If you are wrong, admit it quickly and emphatically.

g. Begin with praise and honest appreciation.

h. Ask questions instead of giving direct orders.

i. Give the other person a fine reputation to live up to.[10]

That's one book you would do well to get out and re-read, and then make it a practice to apply it's concepts in your leadership style and communication.

2. Becoming an effective listener

Effective listening skills are extremely important in communication, as well. In fact, great leaders are great listeners. Listening is definitely a part of people skills; however, in network marketing you'll have to listen so much that we wanted to set this out as a separate skill for your review. There is an abundance of material out there to help you in

---

10   Dale Carnegie, *How to Win Friends and Influence People*, Self-Improvement-eBooks.com, http://images.kw.com/docs/2/1/2/212345/1285134779158_ht-wfaip.pdf (accessed 6/19/17).

this area. Here are ten excellent listening tips from an article on forbes.com called "10 Steps to Effective Listening"[11]:

a.   Face the speaker and maintain eye contact.

b.   Be attentive, but relaxed.

c.   Keep an open mind. Listen without jumping to conclusions.

d.   Listen to the words and try to picture what the speaker is saying.

e.   Don't interrupt and don't impose your "solutions."

f.   Wait for the speaker to pause to ask clarifying questions.

g.   Ask questions only to ensure understanding.

h.   Try to feel what the speaker is feeling. Empathy is the heart and soul of good listening.

i.   Give the speaker regular feedback.

j.   Pay attention to what *isn't* said—to nonverbal cues. If you exclude email, the majority of direct communication is probably nonverbal.

3.   Becoming a problem solver

Another skill you need as a leader is problem solving. How you resolve conflicts really defines you as a leader. When something challenging or negative is presented to you in front of your organization, the entire group watches you intently to see how you will react and handle the problem.

4.   Strategies for communicating with your team

As a leader, you need to develop strategies on how to communicate with your entire organization, with your inner circles, and with the next generation of leaders that's

---

11   Dianne Schiling, "10 Steps to Effective Listening," forbes.com, https://www.forbes.com/sites/womensmedia/2012/11/09/10-steps-to-effective-listening/#705751393891 (accessed 7/6/17).

coming up through your group. You'll have to think about how you communicate differently with each group—how to speak to them where they are —whether it's through phone calls, conference calls, live video, recorded video, audio, email, text, or social media posting. In most cases you will end up doing a little bit of everything; however, be careful not to do too much. Yes, you can distract your team with too much communication. For example, having a team conference call every night between 7 and 9 p.m. would virtually pull your group out of prime-time building every night of the week. They would be informed, and yet they would not have time to grow their business.

You'll also need to find your rhythm for communicating with the different groups. How often do you need to communicate? How much is too much? And how should you communicate with each group?

Here is a general outline for balanced communication:

Frequency	Activity	Purpose
Daily	Post to social media	Recognition, announcements, updates, and training
Daily	Provide personal development and/or team trainings and encouraging your team to listen to them	Team growth
Two to three times a week	Emails	Recognition, announcements, updates, and training
Weekly	Inner circle call	High level discussion and information
Weekly	Team call/video training	Pulling everyone together for updates, motivation, recognition, and training
Monthly	Leadership live call/video	Motivation, inspiration, instruction
As needed (no more than once a day)	Texting	Variety

Of course this is just a basic outline. The company may handle some of it, and you, as a leader, will need to fill in the gaps. If you want to create the right culture for your team—a culture that makes them feel like they're part of something—you need to make sure they receive the proper communication.

5. Communicating for personalities

As a leader, you need to know how to communicate according to personality style, which we alluded to earlier in this chapter. We both recommend using the DISC Personality Profile (see the online store at tonyjeary.com for our specialized version) to determine someone's primary personality style, which will help you understand them better and know how to communicate with them in a way they can best receive your message. Remember, network marketing is a people business; it's built on relationships. If you really want to leverage your relationships, communicate and connect with people the way they want it.

> **Personality Style:**
> Knowing someone's primary personality style will help you understand them better and know how to communicate with then in a way they can best receive your message

Understanding these personality types is really a strategy in maximizing your impact as a leader. We highly recommend that you take a course on this subject. Often when I (Ryan) sit down with leaders, they aren't even aware of their own personality type. They don't know their own strengths and weaknesses. As you develop your inner circle of top leaders, you'll find that different things motivate different people. You will want to think through this as you run promotions and one-on-one counseling sessions. You can learn to communicate with people almost instantly, based on their personality; and usually within five minutes of meeting someone you'll know how to deal with them. In reality, this skill helps you deal with the frustrations that normally accompany leadership and dealing with people. You'll be able to more easily accept them for who they are and help them grow into better people and leaders, based on how they develop naturally.

☐ A "D" personality is a driver, a personality that wants results. "D" personalities don't want the details; they make decisions based on results and speed. They want everything to be fast-paced, and they just want to see the bottom line. Don't give that type of person all the details and drag things out; just give them the bottom line up front.

☐ An "I" personality is an influencer, a personality that likes to build relationships. They like to be social. Often an "I" is persuasive and warm. They want people to support their ideas and opinions, and they want to be recognized. If you get down to the bottom line too quickly and don't socialize with them, you're probably missing a connection in that relationship.

☐ An "S" personality is steady and nurturing. They care about taking care of others and being very service-oriented. They want to talk feelings, not facts. They want approval, and they don't like to be backed into a corner. This personality type wants to know where they're going. You can help this person by showing them the steps and how the choices will lead you together.

☐ A "C" personality is very compliant, cautious, and detail-oriented. They are analytical problem solvers and detail-oriented. They like to perfect processes and work plans. The more systematic and logical, the better for them. Their high expectations of themselves and others can at times be critical. If you have someone like that on your team, communicate the details and give that person time to digest them.

Make sure you understand the specific styles of the people on your team and communicate accordingly.

Communicating well goes a long way toward your success as a leader in network marketing. If you put these communication principles and ideas to work, you'll see a dramatic difference in your results.

Trust

Strategy No. 18 VIP: If you have to question anything, you have to question everything.

High Performance Teams trust each other. If you want to build an organization that's sustainable, then you're going to have to work together in a culture of trust. And in order to build that culture in your network-marketing business, you have to build your organization from a position of values and ethics.

Let me (Ryan) be frank for a moment: There are a lot of people who are making money in network marketing that I wouldn't want to be in business with, because I don't trust them! Yes, they have a knack for doing enough work to get some momentum going in a few teams, and yet their entire downline doesn't even like them! That's the anomaly of network marketing.

Trust equals credibility. Period. When you decide the type of person you want to be known as, "trust" becomes a very important word. Trust is more than just honesty. You don't have to be a liar for someone not to trust you. If they can't trust how you're going to react, even if you're not lying, they're not going to tell you the things you need to hear. You may remember a statement I made in chapter one: If you have to question anything, you have to question everything.

Rights versus Responsibilities

So how do you develop trust within your team? Here's a good way to illustrate this for network-marketing purposes, and it's a thought I (Ryan) know I stole from someone (I just don't remember who). It's another "versus": Rights versus responsibilities. Leaders live in a fish bowl of judgment. Everyone is watching. The higher the responsibility you have in an organization, the fewer rights you have. As you move up in your organization, if you want to be viewed as a top leader, then you lose the right to complain publicly. You lose the right to overact, because everything you do gets magnified that much more. You lose the right to edify the wrong people. If you do any of those things, you're not going to have credibility with your team.

Your team must be able to trust you at all times and in all circumstances. They must trust:

1. Your decision making (do you vet things through your inner circle?)

2. That you are looking out for them

3. That if you make a mistake, you will own it

4. That everyone will be treated fairly

5. That you will do everything in your power to deliver what is expected

Leaders carry a lot of responsibility; and when you carry out well the responsibilities of accountability, communication and trust, you'll be a *High Performing Leader* (HPL) with a *High Performing Team* (HPT) that will outperform your wildest expectations.

In the last chapter, we're going to pull it all together for you and show you how to reach the level of mastery in each of the strategies we've covered so far in the book, as well as give you three additional strategies to help get you over the top.

VIPs

☐ *High Performing Team: A High Performing Team* works together to get the very best results, and they continually reevaluate to make sure they produce the best quality.

☐ *High Performing Leader:* When you truly hold yourself accountable, employ proper communication, and are trusted by your followers, then and only then will you be a *High Performing Leader.*

☐ Accountability: The leadership side of accountability is far more effective than the management side of accountability.

☐ Leadership versus Management: Leadership is inspiring your team and showing them direction. Management can be similar to babysitting them to make sure they're doing what they say they're going to do.

☐ Communication: Intentional communication (understanding the who, what, how, how much, and how often) categorizes your level of leadership more effectively than any other skill in your arsenal.

☐ Life is a Series of Presentations: Life is a Series of Presentations. Every encounter you have, you're *presenting* yourself and you're *representing* yourself and/or your business.

☐ Personality Style: Knowing someone's primary personality style will help you understand them better and know how to communicate with them in a way they can best receive your message.

☐ Trust: If you have to question anything, you have to question everything.

Self-Evaluation

On a scale of 1 to 5, with 5 being the highest, rate yourself on the five issues below to determine where you stand as a leader:

1. I am a *High Performing Leader* and I have created a *High Performing Team.*

2. I effectively use the leadership side of accountability rather than the management side. I'm great at leading by relationships.

3. I set the example for my team with my aggressive personal development plan and by intentionally filling my calendar with the right things.

4. I am a master communicator. I have great people skills, and I effectively use the communication skills set out in this chapter.

5. I have created a culture of trust in my organization from a position of values and ethics.

## Chapter Seven

Mastery

The master in the art of living makes little distinction
between his work and his play, his labor and his leisure,
his mind and his body, his information and his recre-
ation, his love and his religion. He hardly knows which
is which. He simply pursues his vision of excellence at
whatever he does, leaving others to decide whether he's
working or playing. To him, he's always doing both.

— *James Michener*

When I (Tony) first read this powerful quote, I had to reread
it several times. In fact, I put it in my phone so I could read
it over and over again. My immediate thought when I first read it
was, *You know, that's where I want to play.* It's a perfect description
of living a life of mastery, and that's where we hope you want to
play, as well.

One thing I've learned in working with so many top achievers
all over the world is this: *The biggest enemy of mastery is greatness.*
Many people live at the good level. Some live at the great level.
Very few, however, move past that and get to the mastery level.
Mastery is a puzzle that requires the right pieces, and we're going
to give you three of those pieces right now.

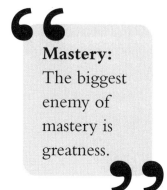

Mastery:
The biggest
enemy of
mastery is
greatness.

When I (Ryan) observe people at the highest levels in the network-marketing industry, I see that they have mentored people and given them enough freedom to grow, to the point that they have duplicated *High Performance Leadership* within their organization. At this point they have been so consistent with who they are that they become known for certain things; and this, in essence, defines their brand. They're no longer thinking about everything they're doing; their habits have become a part of who they are. This is what mastery looks like.

Now let's look at these three pieces of mastery in network marketing—mentorship, your brand, and habits—in more depth.

Strategic Networker Strategy No. 19

Mentorship

Strategy No. 19 VIP: Your ability to mentor the right people will ultimately determine the culture and size of your impact.

Every leader knows that our industry is about the art of duplication, and those who succeed the most at the top level have mastered this art. You reach the mastery level in mentoring when you become what I (Ryan) have termed a "mentor maker"—when through your influence you inspire, grow, and attract like values in a way that promotes others to become mentors. At that point, the people you have mentored have, under your influence, become an

> **Mentor Maker:** You reach the mastery level in mentoring when you become a "mentor maker"—when through your influence you inspire, grow, and attract like values in a way that promotes others to become mentors.

extension of you. There is complete trust, they know how you think, and you know how they think. Your values are set in stone, and your brand is defined by your habits in the first six sections we've talked about in this book.

If we were to guess, we would say that most of you reading this book probably don't currently have a mentor in your life. As a matter of fact, when I (Tony) am making a presentation to large groups, I ask people to raise their hands if they have a mentor, and usually only around three or four percent do. I think a huge *Blind Spot* in all of life is that most people don't make mentorship a strategic component of their lives. They don't have mentors to help them be their best, and they don't think about mentorship as a key way to help others win. Most of us get and give a measure of "unintentional" mentoring through life; however what we're suggesting is that you become strategic about it.

Leadership versus Mentorship

All leaders are not mentors. Leadership is who you are and what you do with an organization. Mentorship, though, is what you do with an individual on a personal, one-on-one basis, where you invest time, energy, and effort supporting that individual. I (Ryan) know that Tony is a leader in the personal development/performance potential industry. And yet, because he invests time supporting me personally, he's also a mentor.

All top leaders should mentor. In fact, I (Tony) have a list, called Leadership 25, of the top twenty-five things a leader at the mastery level should do, whether they are a CEO or running their network-marketing business. Item No. 17 on the list is mentorship, which I often find is missing with top leaders. They're not strategic about mentoring the up-and-comers and supporting them so that they have bench strength underneath them. An exceptional leader is always thinking, *How do I mentor those underneath me?*

Advice Matters

In 2016 I (Tony) co-authored a book with my friend and business mentor Jay Rodgers called *Advice Matters*, based upon the premise that a wise person learns from both the successes and mistakes of others. Jay and I both believe, as does Ryan, that that principle has shaped our lives and careers probably as much as any other, because we've witnessed its power firsthand over the years. Learning strategically from the wisdom and insight of others helps us to be more successful *faster.*

Seeking advice from others who have achieved the kind of results you're looking for is one of the wisest—and quickest—ways to design and live a successful life, grow your business, and hit that next level of success you've been endeavoring to reach. In fact, seeking advice is often the crucial piece of the success puzzle that catapults your results into an arena you could never have achieved alone. Learning from the experiences of others, both their mistakes and their successes, helps you think better and thus leads to better decisions, a better business, and a better life. Wise advice can also help you avoid pitfalls that could derail your success.

> **Advice Matters:** Seeking advice from others who have achieved the kind of results you're looking for is one of the wisest—and quickest—ways to design and live a successful life, grow your business, and hit that next level of success you've been endeavoring to reach.

One of the most important things to remember in getting advice is that the results you get from that advice will be a direct reflection of the credentials and expertise of the source. If you get good advice, you'll get good results; and if you get great advice, you'll get great results. What you really want, though, is mastery advice, because the transition from great to mastery has a colossal impact on your results. Mastery advice comes from someone who's been down the road you want to travel, experienced it, created it, lived it, and has a track record of exceptional results.

When most people consider seeking advice to help them make wise decisions and improve their results, they primarily think of coaches and mentors. In the book *Advice Matters*, we proposed that there are actually six sources of advice available:

1. Coaches

2. Mentors

3. Trusted colleagues

4. Paid professional advisors (attorneys, CPAs, etc.)

5. Resources (like books, videos, and URLs)

6. Yourself (self-reflection)

My definition of a coach is basically a paid mentor. And an excellent coach is a paid mentor with a toolbox. If you want to be an exceptional mentor to others, then, be sure to bring your tool box to the table. By that I mean you need to collect an arsenal of tools to give to those you mentor, such as the resources we mentioned above—books, videos, URLs, and any other tools that would support the person you are mentoring—that allow you to leverage and duplicate more effectively.

Mentoring on the Mastery Level

At the mastery level, you generally want to invest your mentorship energy into top leaders who have performed and can continue to perform at a higher level. I (Ryan) often see people in my organization who could potentially go to another whole level if I could spend some one-on-one time mentoring them. However, there are certain criteria they have to meet. You want to be selective and pour your time into those who are not only proven but who are also receptive to your mentoring.

When you find a person who qualifies, you might go to them and say, "I can see you have a track record that deserves my attention to mentor you in a special way," and then start pouring your energy into them accordingly. When you invest time with someone and they don't respond to what you're saying, though, that can happen only a few times before you must move on. Even if that person really does have potential, they have to be ready for mentoring before you can allow yourself to continue. Remember, you need to model duplication. The five or ten people you're mentoring need to be able to pick up on your cues—what you do and how you do it—and duplicate it themselves.

Another nuance here is that you're not trying to get everyone to be just like you. Of course, you might sometimes wish more could be like you; and yet,

Mastery-Level Mentoring: At the mastery level, you generally want to invest your mentorship energy into top leaders who have performed and can continue to perform at a higher level.

they're never going to be, because they haven't done your life. They haven't lived in the same places; they don't have the same parents; and they don't have the same personality, the same discipline, the same motivations, or the same histories. Every company has a system, and being able to duplicate and mentor people to use their personalities, backgrounds, and motivations to use that system is a sign of mastery. Mentoring a diversity of others and supporting the duplication of the system that works so it can be duplicated again is what makes the magic happen in this business.

Actually, this book is a mentoring book. It's written to leverage our mentorship with you, the reader, because we can't pour into all of you personally. And in reality, at the mastery level the twenty-one strategies in this book should be the basis for the majority of the mentorship conversations you have with people in your organization. In other words, you're going to end up talking about *Strategic Mindset*, clarity, focus, execution, force multipliers, leadership, and mastery—and the three strategies within each category—on a continual basis. These seven areas and twenty-one strategies are really designed for the person who is already successful in the industry and who wants to be mentored to another level—all the way to mastery.

Rewards of Mentoring

At the mastery level, you have allowed and continue to allow yourself to be mentored; however, much of your time is now invested with *High Performance Leaders,* helping them to continue to develop their thinking. This is truly where the long-term business thinker excels, and it's where there is a greater chance of a lifetime of rewards. You have likely earned many financial rewards attaining mastery, and yet this is a different type of reward. This is a legacy reward and a respect reward—rewards that money really can't buy.

Your Brand

Strategy No. 20 VIP: Your strategic presence, or your brand, has a huge impact on how people are attracted to and follow your lead.

What are you known for? What is your top strength? Most people don't strategically develop their brands; they just let their reputations play themselves out. If you want to lead at the mastery level, we suggest you be strategic about building your brand.

People often think of a brand as business cards, clothing, a website, or other materials that have been created to represent someone. Actually, all of these are only *part* of a brand. Your brand is really defined as how the world views you and what you value. So in reality, a successful network-marketing brand is really a representation of who you are. It's your unique promise.

Build a brand based not only on the kind of leader you want to be, but also on who you actually are and the core of how you live today. People want to do things with people they trust and respect. They want to follow people who care. They want to know you will get the job done. They want to know you bring value to their world. We all have a brand. Top leaders are intentional about building theirs.

Think about your brand and determine specifically how you want to be known. Then strategically build it out and leverage it every way you can. Once your trusted brand is in motion, then certainly the websites and cards can be created; however, these are only a representation of what your brand stands for.

I (Tony) believe one of the reasons that Ryan has been so successful in network marketing is because he's put great energy into creating a brand that identifies him as a person who follows through on time and does what he says he's going to do. He personifies a master leader in every way.

> **Network-Marketing Brand:** Your brand in network marketing is an accumulation of everything you believe and do, both personally and professionally.

I was negotiating a deal last weekend; and in preparation, my attorney sent an email saying that he has known me for thirty years and helped me negotiate a lot of my deals. He said in all those years I've always been more than fair in my negotiations. He was validating a part of my brand.

Your brand in network marketing is an accumulation of everything you believe and do, both personally and professionally. It's based on not only how you build your business, but also your leadership style, your personality, your organizational method, and the way you communicate—in essence, how you live out the twenty-one strategies in this book.

Standards of Excellence

If you want to advance to the mastery level, you have to get this distinction right. Period. Cultures are built around standards. People are continually deciding whether they want to be a part of your brand. The bottom line is this: Whatever you do, day in and day out, it's going to become part of how people see you. In essence, at the mastery level, your standards of how you operate, who you are, becomes your strategic presence, or your brand. And at this level, the stronger your brand, the more good things you will attract.

Personal standards not only guide you into making the best decisions on your journey to mastery; they also set the stage for minimal distractions and help you say no more often so you can get rid of *Low Leverage Activities*. Do you want to live in mastery? If so, make sure you've thought through all these pieces.

Let me (Tony) share with you my twelve personal standards— twelve specific things I do every day, which I believe are reflected in my brand:

1. Each morning, pray for wisdom. I start each morning in prayer.

2. Do team huddles or stimulate huddles for my team. Each morning I line up my team, either by phone, e-mail, or in person, and we huddle about all the things we need to do that day. Even if I'm traveling, I'll send a note by email and my team will huddle without me, using the e-mail I sent. I believe incredible synergy comes from doing team huddles, and many leaders miss that.

3. Glance at my new business opportunities to keep them fresh in my mind. My relationship manager sends me an email every morning, and I look at it and think about the opportunities that are ahead of me. I want to keep those fresh in my mind every day so I have it down tight.

4. Determine my top priorities for the day or the week. We have a master to-do list that we look at every day and determine the top priorities. I look at the master list to see what my personal priorities are, because throughout the day I want to make sure I'm doing the things that are at the top of my list. How about you? Do you get down in the weeds too much, or do you lift up and really zoom in on your priorities? Remember what we said earlier in the

book: It's not about activity; it's about productivity. (See my YouTube video on this subject at https://www.youtube.com/watch?v=FqKRadngkHw.) At the end of the day I want to know that I got the most important things done—not that I just got a ton of things done.

5. Touch my family and my team members inspirationally in some way. That means I get up in the morning and love on my wife by sending her a note or smiling and saying nice things to her when she walks into the kitchen. If my kids are home, that means I'm loving on them. When I walk into my studio I want to have a smile on my face and be inspirational to my team. How about you? Are you committed to being the type of leader who impacts everyone you touch each day?

6. Compliment and communicate appreciation for those around me. I am convinced that many people miss this one. When is the last time you heard someone say, "Would you quit appreciating me?" Probably never, because everyone wants to be appreciated. Right? People crave appreciation.

7. Stretch, flex, and breathe with both confidence and gratitude. I want to keep my body healthy, and I want to appreciate everything I have. Gratitude makes me a better person.

8. Organize and rationalize to keep things clean. (Be a river, not a reservoir.) If you were to look at my closets, you would see that they're clean. And the same with my car. I'm constantly giving things away to get them out of my life and keep things clean and organized. Clutter sucks your energy, and keeping things organized and tight frees your mind and energy for bigger and better things.

9. Visualize my own goals (short and long term) with focus and clarity. What you have real clarity about and focus on

is what you execute. I visualize everything, and I study my visioning tools every day.

10. Model exceptional behavior, including enjoying life. How many people fill their lives with all kinds of cool things and then don't enjoy life? I encourage you to stop and enjoy the moment. If you have sunshine, enjoy the sunshine. If you have rain, find ways to enjoy the rain. I want to love and enjoy every single day of my life. How about you?

11. Eat healthy. I have my team make sure nothing gets in front of me that's not healthy, because I get tempted just like everyone else does. I don't want unhealthy food in my pantries or refrigerators. I want every food I see to be healthy. In the last section of this chapter, we'll be talking about habits, and one of my strategic six is the habit of staying healthy. It's right up there among the six habits I think will contribute the most to my success.

12. Doing favors for those who are a part of my life. I make giving gifts an important part of my life. I handwrite notes and send them to hundreds of people a year; I email out best ideas to people; and when I find videos I think are valuable, I send the links to people. I'm constantly doing favors for others so I can help them be their best. How about you? Do you make doing favors for others a standard in your life?

There you have my twelve personal daily standards that help me live a life of mastery. It's not about perfection. It's about holding yourself to high standards if you want to reach mastery with your personal brand.

High standards of excellence are what continue to make *High Performance Leaders* want to be part of an organization or brand.

While Tony's performance standards are daily habits (behaviors) that reinforce his values and help him maintain a high standard of excellence, my (Ryan's) top ten values are my standards of excellence. In essence, my values are the filters I measure my performance by, both in my business and in my personal life. They are my brand; they define who I am and what I want to be known for. For example, honesty is one of my top ten values; and because I want people to see me as honest in both the good and the bad times, that's the standard I hold myself to at all times and in all circumstances.

> **"**
>
> **Standards of Excellence:**
> High standards of excellence are what continue to make *High Performance Leaders* want to be part of an organization or brand.
>
> **"**

Really, it's a two-way street. Your standards are reflected in your brand, which attracts like-minded leaders to you. At the same time, your performance standards help you become more conscious of who you should spend time with. Whether they're more behavior-oriented like Tony's or more filter-oriented like mine, they reflect the values you live by. You wouldn't want to invest time with anyone whose values are not congruent with yours, because they would obviously not support the standards you live your life by. When you have personal standards of excellence, then, who you allow yourself to invest time with is now dictated by who you want to invest time with.

The bottom line is, you want to make sure the brand you present to the world represents the *High Performance Leader* you are and attracts other *High Performance Leaders* to follow you all the way to mastery.

Habits

Strategy No. 21 VIP: Acquire patterns of behavior that often lead to the proven outcomes you desire.

Mastery happens when intentional becomes habit—when you no longer have to think about those things you used to have to be intentional about. In this book, we're teaching you how to be intentional at a higher level. When that becomes automatic—when it becomes a part of who you are and you have the results to prove it—you've arrived at mastery, and people are going to want to follow you.

For decades I (Tony) have worked with and advised the best masters across industries all over the world; and I've come to believe that there are three basic steps to becoming a master at any facet of your life:

☐ Step one: You have to be aware of the different levels (good, great and mastery) and know in what level you are operating.

☐ Step two: You must understand the benefits of living at the mastery level so your "want-to factor" kicks into high gear. Then you are self-inspired and motivated because you truly understand the feelings you can experience by living at this success level.

☐ Step three: *You must execute to the point of habit, where the right things (in both thinking and doing) become automatic. Your habits allow you to produce incredible results over and over.*

Habits are powerful, and they're a huge part of the mastery puzzle. Developing good habits allows you to master the things in life that are important to you and helps you weed out bad habits. The bottom line is, good habits make you more productive and set you up to better succeed.

> **"** **Automatic:** You must execute to the point of habit, where the right things (in both thinking and doing) become automatic. Your habits allow you to produce incredible results over and over. **"**

I (Ryan) often say when I'm counseling someone in the network-marketing industry, "They may not be happy with them, but people are getting the exact results they should be getting, based on the habits they've developed."

If you're not getting the results you want, then, there's a pretty simple solution. Notice I didn't say "easy"; developing the right habits can often be difficult. Most people overcomplicate this issue, though, because there aren't that many habits you have to develop to reach the mastery level in this business. And since you probably already have a number of good habits, you likely just have to get really good at a few more.

For example, Tony has six strategic habits that he focuses on, which we'll share with you later in this section. Now, he has quite a few other really good habits that are derived from those six, and yet it's not like he has to focus on 175 habits every day. Most of Tony's habits have become automatic as he has focused on the six.

Intentionally Develop Strategic Habits

Research shows that 40 percent of our lives are made up of habitual activities. I (Tony) would like to keep mine at 60, 70, or even 80 percent, and this is what I teach people who want to live in mastery.

You may remember in chapter five we talked about the basal ganglia at the center of our brain that looks for patterns (habits) so it can offload them from the cerebral cortex (the "thinking" part of the brain) and free up RAM in that part of our brain for other things. In other words, the basal ganglia grabs and stores the habits that have become automatic because we no longer need to think about them. People who live in mastery have developed habits that automate many things in their lives.

If you want to be a master network marketer, then, you have to be strategic about moving things into the automatic zone (the basal ganglia). By taking full advantage of that function of your brain and more intentionally developing the habits that will move you toward mastery, you will be able to put your efforts and energies where you want them. The habits you create will be modeled in your brand, and they will also support all of the other strategies in this book.

> **Expected Results:** They may not be happy with them, but people are getting the exact results they should be getting, based on the habits they've developed.

Tony's Strategic Six Habits

I (Tony) deploy six strategic foundational habits that help me live in that mastery level. I want to share these strategic six with you right now:

1.   Strategic list making and list managing. You can release things from your mind when you put them down in a list, because you know you can go back and look at them later. I consider this one of my magic habits. I carry my two phones with me almost twenty-four hours a day and make my lists—including my HLAs, my goals, my spouse's goals, and my *Life Team,* among many others—so I'm able to execute at a higher level.

> **Basal Ganglia:** If you want to be a master network marketer, you have to be strategic about moving things into the automatic zone (the basal ganglia).

2.   Strategic goal-setting. I believe you've seen through this book that I'm very intentional about goal-setting. If you want to live in mastery, it's crucial that you make goal-setting one of your strategic habits.

3.   Strategic health. We can have everything in the world, and yet if we don't have our health, does it really matter? And because I previously had a *Blind Spot* in this area, I have now put living healthy as a habit—a lifelong habit.

4.   Strategic learning. I meet very few people that study more than I do. Almost every night, I read and watch videos that will help me learn. I often go to bed watching bios, because I like to hear about other people's success stories and learn their distinctions.

5.   Strategic altruism. That's being automatic about constantly encouraging, supporting, helping, and doing things for others. I like to help others win.

6.   Strategic willpower. Willpower is like a muscle. It can grow big, and it can get tired. With the right management it can be strengthened to positively impact your decisions, like the decision to eat correctly. I want to be smart about my willpower, because I know I get weak, as everyone does, as the day goes on.

Those are the six areas I personally want to continue to thrive in, because those are the habits I believe will support my ability to continue living in mastery.

Habits to Duplicate and Habits to Avoid

In chapter two we talked about setting goals in the six areas of the balance wheel of life: financial/business, physical/health, home and family life, educational, social, and spiritual. What better way to achieve mastery in each of those life areas than to develop strategic habits that support those goals? However, there are also habits that you must intentionally avoid if you want to achieve mastery in those areas. We've identified for you below two habits in each area that we're suggesting would be to your advantage, and two that you must avoid:

Habits to Develop and Habits to Avoid in the Balance Wheel of Life		
Category	**Habits to Develop**	**Habits to Avoid**
Financial/ Business	Saving at least 10% every month and building a nest egg Studying how money works	Accumulating unneeded debt Spending without smart thought
Physical/ Health	Eating smartly Exercising smartly (balance, stretching, resistance and cardio)	Stressing over situations, people, etc. Getting too little sleep
Home and Family Life	Investing time in your family Modeling right habits	Complexing Holding grudges

Continued

Continued

Educational	Reading/studying every single day Investing time being mentored	Not asking for inputs Hanging on to old thinking
Social	Investing time with those who matter (you can pour into them and they can positively influence you) Experiencing the world	Using limited thinking Holding onto relationships that are not productive
Spiritual	Praying every day Ministering to others daily	Keeping an overwhelming schedule Being too inward

The bottom line is that our lives are filled with habits—good and bad. If your results in life point directly to your habits, then obviously they're very important. Certainly each of you reading this book is at a different point in your life and business; and yet no matter where you are, you can each evaluate the habits that are working for you or against you (MOLO) and make slight adjustments so you can potentially arrive at mastery in many areas.

I (Ryan) personally review the balance wheel of life annually to help me focus on new habits in each of the six areas that can re-enforce the life I want. I have found that within a few months to a year, anyone can improve habits to the point where many will become second nature (automatic). When that happens, it's time to add a new habit in that area that will help lead you toward mastery. Some habits will come more naturally than others and will require less work; however, if you don't focus on them, they will never take hold.

Let me give you a few network-marketing habits that have specifically had a huge impact on me and my business:

1. Think before I answer when communicating with leaders, and never answer when I'm upset. In my earlier years, I would often answer quickly to tough questions; and although leaders should learn how to think on their feet, this didn't always serve me well. I have learned that when

problems present themselves, it's often best to say, "Let me process this for a bit, and I'll get back with you." Then seek counsel or simply sleep on it. More often than not, you'll have a more thoughtful answer that will serve the situation much better for the long term.

2. Fill my calendar first, before others fill it. That includes weekly and monthly meetings and events, as well as family time, church time, friend time, and recreational time. You have to learn to own your calendar, or you will constantly be behind the eight ball.

3. Read or listen to at least one book each month. Very few people stretch themselves to grow consistently, and that habit keeps me in the one percent arena. It also gives me fresh material to share when I'm speaking to groups. It really is a way to become a master in many things simultaneously.

4. Make lists and notes before every leadership meeting or conference call as to what I wanted to accomplish. If you want to be productive with your meetings or conference calls, then make a list of the three to five things you absolutely need to accomplish. It could be announcements, motivation, or a teaching. Then once you've accomplished the list, get off the call or out of the meeting. This habit will cause you to be viewed as someone who is in charge and knows what they're doing.

5. Go to sleep at night with every email, phone call, or needed communication completed: Now this one might seem complicated, and yet it's really not. I read the book *Getting Things Done* by David Allen several years back, and one of the key principles was keeping everything cleaned out and organized regarding your communications and tasks. That's where I learned how to make sure my inbox was emptied each and every night. Here's how I do it: When

I check my emails throughout the day, I make a decision on each email. I will either (1) respond to it immediately, or (2) move it into an action folder where I will respond when I have time. If I determine that I need time, then I respond to the email to let the person know when I'll be addressing the issue. The bottom line is, we don't realize how much stress we create for ourselves by not cleaning out our communications and leaving things hanging in the back of our minds.

6. Always follow up within twenty-four hours of a presentation or meeting with key contacts. The truth is that most sales are lost in the follow up. Even if the person has no intention of signing up or doing business with you right away, view the follow up as a seed planted for the future. And you never know what the future holds. You can, however, control whether or not people remember you as professional.

We've identified below two habits in relation to each of the six sections of this book that you will want to develop in your network-marketing business as you're striving for mastery, as well as two habits you'll need to avoid in each area. In the "Habits to Develop" column you'll find habits of the high performers who are on a trajectory course toward the highest level, and in the "Habits to Avoid" column you'll find habits that you must eliminate if you want to live in mastery. There will be other habits you'll want to develop, of course; however, this list will hopefully give you a jumpstart to get you on your way.

	Habits to Develop and Habits to Avoid That Support Each Section in This Book	
Section	**Habits to Develop**	**Habits to Avoid**
Strategic Mindset	Viewing everything you need for mastery as a skill and seeking answers from qualified mentors Constantly checking for and uncovering *Blind Spots*, especially in the five areas of belief for network marketing	Giving excuses for why you aren't good at something Counseling with people who haven't been where you want to go
Clarity	Consistently checking goals against values to ensure alignment Turning every dream into a goal by attaching a proper strategy to make it a reality	Allowing yourself to be pressured to go after something because someone else asks Having strategic conversations and not taking notes
Focus	Doing the MOLO exercise on a regular basis to ensure you stay on track Focusing hourly on your *High Leverage Activities*	Taking on too many projects without judging the time commitment involved Constantly feeling the need to stay busy, whether it's productive or not
Execution	Maintaining a posture that naturally transfers dream and belief Consistently doing the right massive action that will create the momentum for success	Begging, pleading, or leaving too many messages for people (chasing them) Wanting great results, but not booking enough activity to justify them
Force Multipliers	Maintaining a proper event mindset Keeping the right tools readily accessible in your car, briefcase, office, etc.	Doing group meetings with only one group Having poor recognition at your events
Leadership	As much as possible, staying on the leadership side of accountability rather than the management side. Consistently sharpening your communication skills	Constantly telling your team to do things that you've never done Making team decisions without communicating with your top leaders
Mastery	Being a consistent and effective "mentor maker" Consistently living out your brand in everything you do	Thinking that because you've made a lot of money, you no longer need to develop better habits Getting lazy with the balance wheel of life and not setting new goals

It is our sincere hope that we've achieved what we set out to do with this book—helping you find that missing piece of the network marketing puzzle that will help you build the massive organization it takes to reach the level you desire. If you put it to work, the information we've presented through the twenty-one strategies in this book will lead you all the way to the level of mastery, enabling you to realize your highest dreams.

VIPs

☐ Mastery: The biggest enemy of mastery is greatness.

☐ Mentorship: Your ability to mentor the right people will ultimately determine the culture and size of your impact.

☐ Mentor Maker: You reach the mastery level in mentoring when you become a "mentor maker"—when through your influence you inspire, grow, and attract like values in a way that promotes others to become mentors.

☐ Advice Matters: Seeking advice from others who have achieved the kind of results you're looking for is one of the wisest—and quickest—ways to design and live a successful life, grow your business, and hit that next level of success you've been endeavoring to reach.

☐ Mastery-Level Mentoring: At the mastery level, you generally want to invest your mentorship energy into top leaders who have performed and can continue to perform at a higher level.

☐ Your Brand: Your strategic presence, or your brand, has a huge impact on how people are attracted to and follow your lead.

☐ Network-Marketing Brand: Your brand in network marketing is an accumulation of everything you believe and do, both personally and professionally.

☐ Standards of Excellence: High standards of excellence are what continue to make *High Performance Leaders* want to be part of an organization or brand.

☐ Habits: Acquire patterns of behavior that often lead to the proven outcomes you desire.

☐ Automatic: You must execute to the point of habit, where the right things (in both thinking and doing) become automatic.

Your habits allow you to produce incredible results over and over.

☐ Expected Results: They may not be happy with them, but people are getting the exact results they should be getting, based on the habits they've developed.

☐ Basal Ganglia: If you want to be a master network marketer, you have to be strategic about moving things into the automatic zone (the basal ganglia).

Self-Evaluation

On a scale of 1 to 5, with 5 being the highest, rate yourself on the five issues below to determine where you are in achieving mastery in your life and business.

1. I consistently mentor the proven top leaders in my organization who are receptive to my mentoring, to the point that I inspire them and help them grow to become mentors to the leaders in their own organizations.

2. I maintain an excellent tool box (arsenal of tools) to give to those I mentor.

3. I have built a brand that accurately reflects who I am and the promise I make to the world, and I am consistent about living out that brand and leveraging it on a daily basis.

4. I have developed personal standards of excellence, and I am consistent about using them to guide my daily decisions and everything I do, to the point that they are reflected in my brand.

5. I have strategically and intentionally developed habits that support my goals in all six areas in the balance wheel of life, and I have developed habits that support the strategies set forth in this book that have put me on a trajectory course toward the mastery level in my network-marketing business.

Conclusion

Where are you on your journey to the top? Isn't it time to cross the finish line?

You know by now that you're holding in your hand the catalyst that will take you there. The strategies set forth in this book have been proven out over and over. Now, for the first time, these seven powerful RESULTS principles and their twenty-one supporting strategies have been put into print just for you—the successful networking leader who wants to go to another level. In this book, we've spoken directly to you, because we know the industry, we know your struggles, and we know the fastest way to overcome those struggles and achieve superior results—faster!

Picture this very possible scenario...

By following the blueprint we've set out for you in this book, you'll become better, period. Think *Strategic Networker*—not just a networker who works more; rather, one who works more strategically.

Your old thought patterns will fall away and your new ways of thinking will ultimately result in a *Strategic Mindset* that will open your mind to the kind of intentional thinking that is common to seven-figure earners in network marketing. In the process, you'll uncover more of those pesky *Blind Spots* that are keeping you from becoming all you can be, you'll improve both your business and effectiveness skills, and you'll start investing your time more wisely.

You should have more clarity than you've ever known when you identify the values you want to live your life by and apply them to your dreams. Then, with the valuable tools we've given you for setting goals that align with those values, you'll be able to achieve those goals faster.

Your focus challenge— the single biggest contributor to failure in network marketing—will virtually disappear when you do these two things: (1) MOLO your life and business to determine what you want more of and what you want less of, and (2) eliminate distractions by focusing on the five *High Leverage Activities* (HLAs) that have already been identified for you. Then by creating three inner circles—your mentors, your business partners, and your *Life Team*—you'll find your highest potential and be able to put all your energy into focusing on your HLAs.

You'll finally be able to define your income—and your legacy—by executing your goals at the mastery level (intentionally getting more of the right things done and getting them done faster). Your positive posture that naturally transfers dream and belief will cause people to want to follow you. There will be non-stop action in your organization in the areas of sponsoring, launching, and driving depth, and that sustained momentum will allow you and your team to experience a leveraged income that can set you financially free.

You'll break out of that bracket where you're currently trapped by driving the system with three powerful force multipliers: life-changing events, tools, and recognition. When people attend your events, they'll come away with a more defined emotional "why" that drives them to build their business. You and your team use will use tools in a way that will create the leverage that ultimately creates your freedom, and people in your organization will be further motivated to build their business because of the recognition you give them that makes them feel significant.

Your leadership effectiveness will likely skyrocket, because you'll be inspiring people through your example to positively do things they otherwise wouldn't do to reach their potential. In other words, you'll become a *High Performing Leader* (HPL) with a *High Performing Team* (HPT). Rather than choosing to manage your team, you'll use accountability wisely by casting the vision of the results you (or they) are looking for, and your team will take them and run with them. Your intentional communication will categorize you as an effective leader, because you will learn how to use people skills, problem solving, strategies for communicating with your team, and personality profiles in a way that will make your team want to grow their business. And you'll be able to build a culture of trust in your organization from a position of values and ethics.

And finally, you'll achieve the level of mastery in your business that will take you all the way to the top. The size of your impact will increase significantly as you become a "mentor maker"—that is, through your influence, you'll inspire, grow, and attract like values in a way that promotes others to become mentors, all through your organization. You'll create a brand that will have a huge impact on how people are attracted to and follow your lead. And you will acquire the right habits that will lead to the outcomes you desire.

Can't you see yourself becoming a more powerful *Strategic Networker*?

We believe in you. You're already a high-level leader, and the person in the scenario we just described could very well be you.

And as you're applying these strategies to become a *Strategic Networker*, we want to be there for you. We understand that each individual will have different needs. You may need one-on-one coaching from one of us, or you may want one or both of us to speak at one of your national events. We invite you to visit our websites, www.tonyjeary.com and www.ryanchamberlin.com, to see our full range of services and offerings.

This book can be your breakthrough! We hope you're able to clearly see the *Strategic Networker* inside of you and use these seven powerful RESULTS principles and twenty-one supporting strategies to make that vision a reality!

Values

_____ Affection	_____ Fun	_____ Personal Improvement
_____ Alignment	_____ Generosity	_____ Personal Salvation
_____ Altruism	_____ Genuineness	_____ Philanthropy
_____ Appearance	_____ Happiness	_____ Power
_____ Appreciated	_____ Harmony	_____ Productivity
_____ Attitude	_____ Health	_____ Recognition
_____ Cleanliness	_____ Honesty	_____ Relationships
_____ Congruence	_____ Humility	_____ Respect
_____ Contentment	_____ Inner Peace	_____ Results
_____ Cooperation	_____ Inspiration	_____ Romance
_____ Creativity	_____ Intimacy	_____ Routine
_____ Education	_____ Joy	_____ Security
_____ Effectiveness	_____ Knowledge	_____ See the World
_____ Efficiency	_____ Lifestyle	_____ Simplicity
_____ Fairness	_____ Loved	_____ Solitude
_____ Faith	_____ Loyalty	_____ Spiritual Maturity
_____ Fame	_____ Motivation	_____ Status
_____ Family	_____ Openness	_____ Wealth
_____ Financial Security	_____ Organization	_____ Winning
_____ Freedom	_____ Personal Brand	_____ Wisdom

Tony Jeary

Tony Jeary is a strategist, thought leader, and prolific author of over forty titles.

For more than two decades, Tony has advised CEOs and other high achievers on how to discover new clarity for their vision, develop focus on their direction, and create powerful execution strategies that impact achievement and results.

Tony has personally coached the most accomplished people in the world, including presidents of: Walmart, SAM's Club, Ford, American Airlines, HP, Firestone, Samsung, and New York Life.

Tony practices the business mantra his father taught him growing up, "*Give Value... Do More Than is Expected.*"

Tony lives and works on his estate in the Dallas/Fort Worth area where his private *Strategic Acceleration* Studio is located.

www.TonyJeary.com

Ryan Chamberlin

Ryan Chamberlin is a network marketing authority, coach, speaker, and author.

Since 1999, Ryan has built large, sustainable organizations in networking and is now recognized as a leading authority in the industry.

Through his books, training programs, and methodologies, he is a top trainer and coach to many seven-figure networking leaders.

He continues to work with companies and their fields to create systems for business and personal growth through a value based philosophy.

Ryan lives and works in Central Florida.

www.RyanChamberlin.com